Price To Scale

Practical Pricing For Your High-Growth SaaS Startup

AJIT GHUMAN

Price to Scale: *Practical Pricing for Your High-Growth SaaS Startup*

Dedicated to my parents.

CONTENTS

PREFACE

Software Pricing is not a new topic. There's a ton of literature out there that covers either theoretical understanding of sophisticated price elasticity and demand curves or bite-sized "practical" blogs with names such as the "5 basic models" or "7 pricing strategies". These provide some insight but, in reality, exist to serve as lead-generation vehicles to persuade the reader to further engage in the consulting services of the company that has authored the article.

A practical end-to-end guide to creating and operationalizing software packaging and pricing has been lacking. This book aims to fill that void.

Pricing is so important that it impacts decisions right from company strategy and product positioning down to day-to-day sales operations. But due to its perceived complexity, both product managers and product marketers tend to avoid integrating it into their regular launch processes, often resulting in last-minute ad-hoc pricing decisions. Often at fast-growing startups, an inefficient pricing model eventually leads to a breaking point where a total, painful pricing overhaul has to be done.

Getting consultants to do this work isn't guaranteed to work either and is often too expensive. Just the other day, I saw the following opinion echoed within a Product Marketing community that I am a member of. A product marketing leader at a top-tier valley startup posted, *"My past company used [well known consulting company] and paid a few hundred thousand dollars and the pricing recommendations they gave killed our ACV, and I had to revamp pricing and rip and replace their recommendation."*

AJIT GHUMAN

In this book, my goal is to arm you, the Founder/PM/PMM/Revenue Leader, with the tools to make the right set of pricing decisions that will best align your company strategy, product positioning and the needs of your market. These decisions are often not just about the price point itself but the preceding elements of packaging, pricing metrics and pricing structures.

The book seeks to keep away from complex analysis for the most part while still gunning for completeness of the exercise. The hope is to cut through the noise and distill a practical and actionable approach on how to effectively and correctly position, package, and price a software product and/or product portfolio.

Learning by Observation - My 'Aha!' Moment on the Importance of Pricing and Packaging

I worked at Medallia for close to five years from 2011 to 2016 in a phase where the company went from bootstrapped to one of Sequoia's then biggest investments in enterprise SaaS, where revenue grew from around 20M to 120M. I saw the company expand out of hospitality as its core industry segment into financial services, retail, and other industries in this high growth environment. I also saw how a very professional enterprise sales team raised ASPs (Average Selling Prices) by a significant degree.

The price of our software could vary manifold between industries, from a few hundred thousand dollars to multi-million-dollar deals. The business school concept of price discrimination becomes very clear when a financial services company pays 3-4x more than a retail company for roughly the same feature-set.

Additionally, with a better value-driven sales process, Medallia's post-VC money enterprise sales team did much better overall than the pre-VC money team. Every step in the sales process tied back to

---

> customer value, changing the conversation from a software 'tool' to a strategic change in the prospect company's direction.
>
> And while even Medallia wasn't perfect in how it went about pricing, it was clear how much impact a value-based pricing model, with the appropriate communication of value, could have on revenue and valuation.

Why Now?

We see exponential growth in Software as a Service (SaaS) companies. Globally, Gartner predicts that by 2021 cloud revenues will total $278 Billion[1]. That is a staggering amount of money.

In terms of market share, SaaS is expected to represent 45% of the total enterprise software market by 2023. SaaS companies are also drawing in major funding in technology today, with notable players occupying seven of the top 10 verticals by venture capital deal activity and three of the top 10 by investments.

As this growth happens, what will separate the winners from the losers is not just the product. The world is littered with excellently engineered products that could not find product-market fit and withered away. At the same time, there are plenty of examples of growing companies that truly have patch-work products that just seem to work well enough, but with the right GTM approaches and a well-aligned price for their chosen buyer, they have managed to find space for themselves.

I hope that the insights from this book can help the next "little startup that could." (*Cultural reference to the children's classic called "The Little Engine That Could"*)

---

1 https://www.gartner.com/en/newsroom/press-releases/2018-09-12-gartner-forecasts-worldwide-public-cloud-revenue-to-grow-17-percent-in-2019

You are probably leaving money on the table

If you are selling Software, the chances are that you have a lot more room to maneuver than you think.

The beauty of Software is that it is generally not a commodity (more the case with b2b than b2c Software), which means the price isn't your buyer's most important consideration.

This also means that increasing your buyer's perception of the value will enable you to raise prices. A well-positioned, packaged and priced product will help you do just that.

Additionally, a mismatch between value delivered and monetized revenue occurs naturally as a startup grows. High-growth software companies tend to obsess initially (*when starting out*) over new logo acquisition (*as they should*), which inherently incents them to not risk pricing too high. As they grow, their brand's strength also grows, and so does their pricing power. This is why companies tend to undergo an overhaul of pricing at each significant growth stage so that they can monetize their added value to the market.

Is this book for you?

This book is for you if you have the onus of drafting or fixing pricing for your company.

This book is also for you if you are the lone ranger Product Manager/Marketer who wants to design pricing for a specific product that you are responsible for.

Finally, this book is also for Execs and/or Founders who have considered hiring an external consultant or expert to do this for their companies.

This book is **not** for you if:

You are looking for a high, e.g., 95%+, precision pricing in the market. This level of accuracy is usually needed when you have a functional pricing and packaging model that can provide incremental optimization. This tends to be the case with established companies that are selling standardized SKUs at scale and tends to be a need at the pre-IPO or post-IPO life cycle where every $ of incremental revenue means a significant impact on the company's valuation. This also tends to be the case with pricing and optimization for fixed inventory products like airline tickets, hotel bookings, and car rentals.

What can you learn from this book?

At a very rudimentary level creating pricing and packaging requires you to make decisions on four key aspects:

1. **Packaging:** What will be your product 'offers'/'packages'?
2. **Pricing Metric:** Which metric or set of metrics will drive your core pricing model?
3. **Pricing Structure:** How will you structure the price that is driven based on the pricing metric?
4. **Price Point:** What specific price point will you charge?

This book will help you get to those four key decisions and guide you on how to operationalize the pricing within your organization.

Here are some key focus areas that this book seeks to untangle and explain:

- Positioning
  - Why positioning is the core to pricing
  - Basics of product positioning
  - Validating positioning before packaging
- Packaging
  - Why packaging matters more than pricing

- — How to package your product for best fit with your customer base
- — Approaches to help you surface maximum product value
- Pricing
  - — The art of selecting the right pricing variable
  - — Options to set the right pricing structure
  - — Quantitative and qualitative pricing research methods
  - — Selecting the price point itself
  - — Special considerations such as expansions and renewals
- Implementation
  - — The bill of materials required to launch pricing in your organization
  - — How to think about a pricing page on your website
  - — The basics of pricing operations
- Monitoring
  - — How to measure the success of your pricing model

Beyond these topics, I aim to offer a wider perspective of how these steps and decisions vary for companies in different stages of growth. I've tried to do this by offering insights from my own experience and the experience of real pricing gurus who have worked on initiatives for companies such as Oracle, Gainsight, Citrix, Mixpanel Rubrik, Verint, as well as from the established pricing consultancy Simon Kucher Partners.

Why listen to me?

I am not a pricing expert with decades of pricing experience. I am a marketer who learned the nuts and bolts of software pricing and packaging by reading, experimenting and talking to other pricing experts. Based on a logical sequence of steps, I increased product ASPs for pricing and packaging at my firm while increasing my sales team's satisfaction with the new pricing model.

I am writing the book that I wanted to read before I commenced on my own pricing journey. The hope is that you can easily understand and easily apply the sequence of steps offered in this book to design your own pricing and packaging without feeling the need to bring in external consultants or feel like this is rocket science. It's not.

CHAPTER 1

How to get to Pricing - The PPP Hierarchy

The first thing to understand is that the scope of a pricing project isn't just about 'pricing.'

This project will require you to confirm, evaluate, or even set product strategy, positioning, and packaging. It will touch multiple teams within your organization: sales, product, marketing, operations, professional services (yes, them too), and finally, the executive team.

One way to build up to the right answer is to consider a pyramid. Where the base is 'positioning,' a middle tier is 'packaging,' and finally, the piece on top is 'pricing.' I call it the PPP hierarchy (see Figure 1). The point is that you can't get to the top of the pyramid without solidifying the layer below.

Often, there is a tendency (especially in the sales team) to think, "Oh, I have seen enough deals, and so I know how to price our product!" - Avoid this tendency! This approach assumes many strategic considerations and could very well mean that you may not see 'the forest from the trees' view, which is required to make this work over the long term and for your entire market.

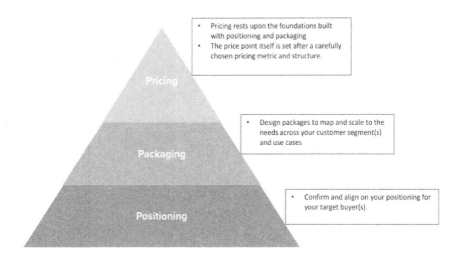

Fig 1: The PPP Hierarchy

This is also why I am somewhat hesitant to bring on external consultants. When you do this exercise internally, not only do you have to evaluate a series of assumptions the company is running under but as you uncover these assumptions, you may change course on strategy.

Furthermore, the collaborative nature of the exercise implies that we would have reached the right approach for the company together, thereby achieving the critical state of "alignment." Alignment ensures buy-in, understanding, and complete adoption of your pricing strategy -- thereby unlocking the incredible leverage of this exercise.

CHAPTER 2

Positioning - Let's start at the very beginning

Positioning is how you carve a place of influence in your buyer's mind.

> l "*Positioning is not what you do to the product; it's what you do to the mind of the prospect. It's how you differentiate your brand in mind. Positioning compensates for our over-communicated society by using an oversimplified message to cut through the clutter and get into the mind. Positioning focuses on the perceptions of the prospect, not on the reality of the brand.*"
>
> - Al Ries, Author of 'Positioning: The Battle for Your Mind.
> Warner Books. 1981

There is a scene in the TV series *Man Men* that has one of the most striking examples of positioning that I've ever seen depicted on screen. If you haven't seen *Mad Men*, I suggest watching the first episode of the first season, or simply search for "*it's toasted mad men*" on Youtube so you can follow along.

As the Creative Head of an advertising firm, the show's protagonist, Don Draper, is charged with repositioning cigarettes for a major client, *Lucky Strike*, when Big Tobacco companies were under considerable fire. There was growing medical evidence that cigarettes were injurious and fatal in many cases. To comply with FDA regulations, tobacco companies had to work on messaging that did not indicate that cigarettes had any health benefits. While Lucky Strike did not have any differentiating element when compared to any of their competitors, what Don Draper did for them was that he focused on Lucky Strike's buyer. He honed in on one part of their manufacturing process: the toasting of tobacco leaves to dry and cure them. He then came up with a simple tagline that said, "It's Toasted."

Here's why this was a stroke of genius by Don Draper:

1. He understood that the cigarette buyer prioritized personal freedom and guilt-free "happiness." He found a position in the buyer's mind that was tied to the smell of sitting in a brand-new car.

2. By saying that it was 'toasted' (which all cigarettes were, but it wasn't a well-known fact), Draper created a perception that sidestepped the health hazards.

3. By using the "it's toasted" call-out, Draper also gave *Lucky Strike* the first-mover advantage. Any competitor who'd come out and say that their cigarette was toasted too would only appear as someone who was emulating and not the pioneer.

4. The 'toasting' done by *Lucky Strike* became an attribute that was now part of the cigarette buyer's bias, and the individual would choose their cigarette over another competitor's owing to the heuristics involved.

Once this position was firmly established in the cigarette buyer's mind, could *Lucky Strike* not have charged a premium for their products? No other brand could elicit a feeling of freedom like *Lucky Strike* could.

Fig 2: Lucky Strike's Advertisement[2]

What I'm trying to point out is that pricing is intimately connected to Positioning. Pricing cannot be set without the Positioning being clearly thought through.

Now let's take an example that's closer to home.

Let's assume for a moment that you are responsible for positioning a new AI-based Sales Productivity software targeting tech company VP of Sales as your buyer persona.

How do we get inside the head of this VP of Sales? How do we 'position' ourselves?

We leverage heuristic thinking.

2 Source: https://bit.ly/3dEpKvz

In his seminal work, *Thinking Fast and Slow*,[3] Nobel Laureate Daniel Kahneman highlights two systems - System 1, which is heuristic, and System 2, which is analytical. A heuristic mindset is like muscle memory for the brain. It enables us to develop micro-second preferences and biases. It's what tells us that an Apple iPhone is a premium product, while an Android phone isn't. It's what makes us hold a BMW in higher esteem in comparison to a Honda, which isn't viewed as a premium product. As the buyer in these cases, we are pegging these products and brands a certain way before taking into consideration the horsepower in a car or the storage capacity of an iPhone.

Coming back to our example, if you approached the VP with a pitch for your product, she is going to run a few heuristics to get a handle on how to think about your product.

There could be three possible heuristics:

1. Vendors she can relate to
2. What do people like her at companies similar to her think?
3. Thought leaders that she follows

While there are thousands of companies in the Sales Tech space, a few companies are seen as the most prominent related to AI. The comparison for your offering will be against these popular companies and their offerings. The VP may compare your company to *Gong, People.ai,* and *Chorus* (see Figure 3).

Apart from the prominent competitors, the VP would also consider what the counterparts in her space, and the people in her network with similar needs, are looking at.

---

3 Thinking Fast and Slow, Daniel Kahneman, 2011

Fig. 3: Understanding the mind space of the prospective customer[4]

She would also look to the opinions of thought leaders in this space and insights from popular podcast platforms such as **Sales Hacker** or **Inside Sales** to help guide her decision.

Once we understand the buyer and their mind space, we can then think about how to find our own niche in that mind space.

There are many questions that arise.

Is your product a 'tool/widget,' or is it a 'platform'?

Is it a vitamin or a painkiller?

How is it uniquely different compared to available alternatives?

What you want is for your buyer to recognize you as a product that solves a particular problem in a differentiated way.

Maybe you already understand Positioning.

---

4   Image source:
https://commons.wikimedia.org/wiki/File:360_Executive_Branding_Founder_Julie_Zu ick.jpg

Why am I bringing it up?

The truth is most pricing problems aren't pricing problems. In fact, they are rarely pricing problems.

They are just the causal impact of poorly understood and/or communicated positioning of a product leading to a lack of conviction and a whole host of downstream issues.

The three essential questions one must always answer to be clear about positioning are:

1. Do we know who our target customer is?
2. What benefit(s) do we bring to her/him?
3. How do we solve her/his problems <u>uniquely better</u> than other alternatives?

A point of clarification: confirming positioning vs. operationalizing positioning

One of the important things to keep in mind is that we are discussing positioning in the context of a Pricing exercise. If this were a pure positioning exercise, you would have to do a lot more in order to operationalize the positioning, and that can include things like influencing analysts, writing research reports, or organizing key domain-relevant events.

When it comes to a pricing exercise, the goal is to understand and confirm the existing positioning of the company and/or a specific product in question (*assuming, of course, that the company has had a working GTM, and this isn't the first time it will be selling an offering*).

The confirmation of the positioning could be as simple as making sure that your understanding of the key buyer personas and the positioning statement roughly matches that of your executive team, sales leadership as well as marketing leadership across every main market-segment that you are targeting.

Real-world example & implications

The criticality of positioning lies in the fact that without clear positioning, no pricing model can work. In fact, without clear positioning your company can fail.

The year is 2018, and I was working for a startup that offered a product for chat-based customer service. At the time, there was a debate on what exactly should be the positioning of our customer support software that primarily worked through a chat widget and via advanced AI-based chatbots.

After examining the market landscape, my boss and I wanted to call our offering a Conversational-AI based Customer Service Platform to highlight the unique differentiator of the product within a large segment of Customer Service software. Our hypothesis was that 'Conversational-AI' would limit our field of competition to one we would do well against.

However, when we brought up this topic with our CEO, who was earlier at a much bigger established company, she disagreed with our approach. Her direction was that we were supposed to be competing with Salesforce and that our eventual destiny was to become a CRM solution. For us (my boss and I), this was totally discordant with the fact that the product was just not a CRM product, and this direction did not address our target buyer or our unique differentiation for that buyer.

This dilemma persisted with the company for quite a while and not only impacted the pricing effort but also slowed down the entire sales engine as the sales team was hearing completely mixed messages (changing every quarter) on who they were to be pitching and what the positioning was in the market.

The point of the story: Before you embark on a pricing exercise, make sure that there is alignment on the positioning within your own company, and if any disagreement exists (especially at the executive level) that it be resolved before you actually work to finalize the pricing.

CHAPTER 3

Packaging: Tailoring your offers

"Price discrimination is important. It means you can charge people based on their propensity to pay. Now, you can't charge people different amounts just because you don't like them. You have to offer them something extra. But it has to be something rich people care about. Business-class seats routinely cost five or ten times more than economy seats. But it costs the airline much less—maybe two or three times more than a standard seat—to provide perks like wider seats, more legroom, and free drinks. A lot of enterprise software companies use price discrimination, especially with freemium products. The free or low-price version will do almost everything you want. But if you want the version that's extra secure or hosted on your site or has multiple-user administration so the IT person can monitor everything, you'll find yourself paying 10 or 100 times more."

– Naval Ravikant[5]

Once you've determined Positioning, the next step is to create 'offers' that will work for your targeted market segments. These offers are the right combination of feature-sets, services, and price for a market

---

5 https://nav.al/rich

segment that will ensure that you can derive the maximum possible value from within that segment.

The set of capabilities in an offer, except the price itself, constitutes a package. In most cases, you will want to create a set of packages that map 1-1 to the number of clearly defined market segments.

Let's use the following figure to understand how packages help.

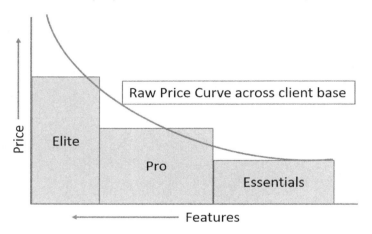

Fig. 4: Graphical representation of Customers' Propensity to Buy and Packages

If we were to draw out a curve that represented how prospects valued a solution when varying the feature-set, we would obtain a curve that looked similar to the one in Figure 4. Intuitively, prospects who need more features (or more advanced features) tend to pay more than prospects who need fewer features. If no pricing model exists, then a time-averaged curve of product ACV (Annual Contract Value) across different customers who had varied usage in features would also look similar.

The goal of establishing a pricing model is to standardize 'packages/offerings' that allow your firm to run a sales engine that helps you achieve a curve like the one above. The curve is maximized for its return from prospects and one that helps you achieve efficiency with your sales engine (via a well-defined pricing model). Unless you sell to a very homogenous set of prospects (e.g., Fortune 100 - Pharma companies), you will want to come up with a packaging structure that lets you capture a progressive amount of value across your customer segments.

What does package look like in everyday life?

Let's lead with a straightforward example of Popcorn (Figure 5). The essential feature that is being charged for is the popcorn itself, and pricing varies based on the quantity offered. This, in essence, is packaging.

The differentiating feature in the packaging is the quantity - Small, Medium, and Large. Customers will pay for the feature they want.

Fig. 5: Popcorn - Packaging

Let us look at another example (Figure 6), that of the Ford Mustang.

Fig. 6: Model Comparison - Ford Mustangs

21

A customer may be looking to buy a *Ford Mustang*. All *Mustangs* are built on a common base, but each model is priced based on the variations in features offered - horsepower, engine specs, shell, interiors, etc.

The sports car aficionado, which is heuristically inclined to associate a *Mustang* as a status symbol, will be willing to spend more and opt for the *Mustang Shelby GT500*. The base model of the *Mustang EcoBoost Fastback* would not have the level of specs that the *GT500* would offer. There would also be discerning customers who want more features than the base model offers but aren't willing to splurge on the most high-end model. The manufacturer assesses this segment as well and offers the *Mustang BULLITT* for them - priced between the base and high-end models. This is a good example of how the manufacturer is looking to maximize the area beneath the curve by offering multiple features of a relatively horizontal product through packaging variations.

This logic applies similarly to software packaging.

So how do you create packages for software?

In my experience, there are roughly two ways to go about this exercise:

1. **Good-Better-Best (GBB):** It is becoming common in SaaS to create 2-3 step graded packages, nicknamed good-better-best packaging, for different customer segments and to map these packages to different price points that those segments will be able to bear. Different sets of features are grouped into a package and targeted at different market segments so as to provide a set of capabilities that do the best job of solving the segment's main use cases. This approach works well in capturing revenue from a market that has a large set of prospects with less variance in their willingness to pay or avg deal size, and often these are SMB and Mid-Market segments. Here deal velocity takes precedence over finely tuned price points.

2. **Modular:** This approach involves attributing value to distinct groupings of features that unlock specific use cases for your prospects. The modularity enables your packaging to vary considerably between any two given customers. This works better in a market where there is a high variance in willingness to pay (WTP) and the average sale price (ASP), and a smaller universe of prospects. In these situations, a high revenue capture rate is more important than velocity. For such cases, flexibility is usually king, and a well-designed, bespoke-fit type of package can help maximize revenue capture in this segment.

The following Figure 6a illustrates roughly how I visualize the decision of selecting a specific approach. A Good-Better-Best model is better suited for when there is a large 'n', i.e., number of customers/accounts available in the market to be sold that are somewhat homogenous in their needs. For example, direct to consumer, digital-first companies in the eCommerce vertical.

On the other hand, the modular approach would be better if the market was more heterogeneous. For example, when the same product is sold to insurance, telco, retail, and/or hospitality where all these industries have varying needs.

When total market 'n' is small, and the market is also heterogeneous. In that case, depending on the circumstance, one can make an argument of creating bespoke packages per client. For example, a selection of 20 top financial issuers with varying use cases for a data science platform.

At the end of the day, there are no rules to this, but hopefully, this helps make your decision process clearer. Once you understand these techniques, you can always mix and match them for the best effect.

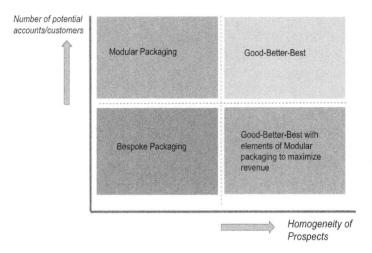

Fig. 6a: Selecting a packaging approach

Good-Better-Best Packaging

In order to understand good-better-best packaging, let's start with the example of Salesforce's Service Cloud pricing[6] (Figure 7):

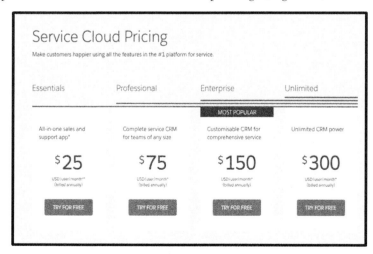

*Fig. 7: **Salesforce** Service Cloud Packages*

---

6 https://www.salesforce.com/products/service-cloud/pricing/

Looking at **Salesforce's** Service Cloud packages, you can see that each package variant provides a range of sub-features that are common, and the higher-priced packages offer more features. In 'Essentials,' they are only going to offer case management. In 'Professional,' they will further offer CRM and case management. CRM is where you can store all your account information, and with just the 'Essentials' package, you may not be able to.

In the 'Unlimited' edition, they offer 24x7 customer support and may offer AI features or some more enterprise features and charge you higher for those impressive or lucrative features that are on offer. This is rudimentary software packaging and pricing.

The packages are graded based on features that map to companies of different sizes and needs (segments). One point of Salesforce's packaging grid is telling. They've clearly outlined on their website what the prices for the different packages are. We can infer from this that Salesforce is trying to achieve a high degree of price standardization and transparency, which tends to be useful when an organization has a large sales engine and a target market that it seeks to attract.

The drawback of such an approach is that prospects can easily comparison-shop to choose the right capability no-matter which industry vertical they are in, making the sales more transactional and missing out on WTP variances between industries, e.g., Financial Services (generally high WTP) vs. Retail (generally low WTP).

Another example is that of a company called Amplitude, which offers product analytics software. Here we can see that Amplitude has three plans[7], one of which is a completely free plan, and the other two seem to be catered to mid-sized growing companies and larger established enterprises, respectively (Figure 8).

---

7 https://amplitude.com/pricing

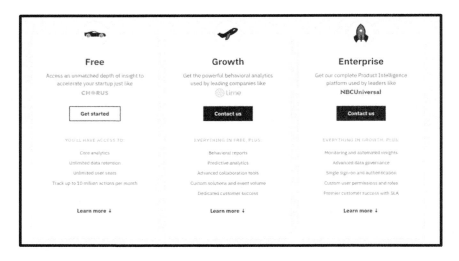

Fig. 8: Amplitude's Pricing Plans

It's interesting to note that they do not expose the pricing for the 'Growth' and 'Enterprise' plans. This indicates that they are going after a broad market across verticals where comparably sized clients might have differing WTP. Not publishing a price allows them to capture greater value from clients that are able to pay more. In the subsequent chapter, we will see how this is accomplished by creative discounting buffers and approval rules for your sales team.

The 'Free' tier offered by Amplitude is another indicator that they intend to reach a wide market, the reason being that 'free' plans have a poor conversion rate in general to paid plans, and the offer would only make sense if a) They were going after a large TAM and/or b) They want to undercut a competitor.

Now, this is not how the pricing page always looked for this company. I always find it interesting to do some research using the Wayback Machine and seeing how a company's Positioning and pricing have evolved. Here are two historical snapshots of their pricing in 2016 (Figure 9).

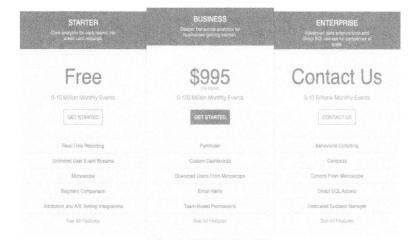

Fig. 9: Amplitude Pricing Plan Evolution

Can we infer anything from the evolution of their pricing page?

I would suggest that what likely happened is as the company found new customers, they realized many of them could pay much more than the company initially charged. Now, this is all well and good since the company in 2016 probably was a new entrant to the market with fewer feature differentiators and less of a brand cache. In 2020, as they innovated with their product and became a more trusted brand, they probably charged more and hence removed the specific pricing from their product page as they didn't want to peg their prices low.

OK, so now that we understand how this type of packaging looks like in real life, how do we create this for our own product?

Well, for one, we know the output of our effort needs to fall into roughly three (or four) packages or tiers. The goal is to bucket features together such that there is:

1. **Gradation:** There is a gradual upward gradation of capability.
2. **Package <> Segment Fit:** Each package's capabilities map to a significant representative market segment that is likely to auto-select a specific package for its needs (i.e., a certain segment always chooses the middle tier, another segment always chooses the bottom-most tier).
3. **No Shelf-ware:** If at the end we find that a certain package is rarely picked by its intended target segment, then that package needs to be removed. Similarly, if we find a package is often selected, but a key underlying feature is unused, then that feature shouldn't be part of the package. *(Read the interview with Johnny Cheng in the case study section of the book to see how poorly fit packages impact a company's sales motion)*

Start by thinking of broad segments of your customers based on your sales motion. One way to do this is by company size and simply use a standard grouping like SMB, Mid-Market, Enterprise. Now create a set of feature groupings such that there is a 1-1 mapping between the feature groupings and the prior defined customer segments.

Here is a fictional example of this exercise for a marketing automation product (Figure 10). We have grouped features to map to our assumed needs for each market segment. The groupings are graded and more complex at the top end.

SMB	Mid-Market	Enterprise
⬆	⬆	⬆
Contact Management	Contact Management	Contact Management
1-5 Users	5-25 Users	25+ Users
Email Editor	Email Editor	Email Editor
Email Support	Advanced Validation Rules	Advanced Validation Rules
	Analytics	Analytics
	Email Support	Data Enrichment
		Dedicated Success Manager

Fig. 10: Packaging our Automation Product

At this point, we have our initial hypothesis of packaging, but this needs to be tested against our selected customer segments to see whether there truly is package <> segment fit. In the next chapter, we will cover research methods to answer this very question.

But before that, let's now take a look at modular packaging.

This discussion brings up an important point on pricing transparency. According to a recent report by Chartmogul,[8] roughly 75% of SaaS companies publish pricing on their websites, and 25% do not. In my opinion, this is interesting data but by no means a reason to follow the herd per se.

I'd like to propose a simple 2x2 matrix (Figure 11) to decide when it would make sense to publish the prices along with the packages on your website.

---

8 https://blog.chartmogul.com/saas-pricing-report/#pricingMatters

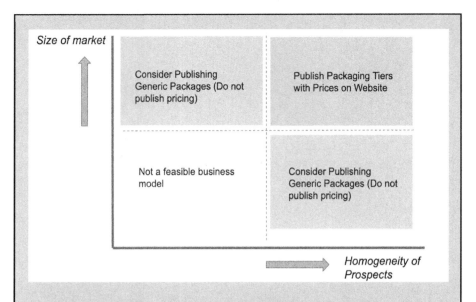

Fig. 11: Deciding on Price Transparency

When you have a large market with a high degree of homogeneity, it is feasible to emulate other SaaS companies and publish the complete pricing structure online (replete with packages and prices) to help you scale your sales engine and maximum value from the market. On the other hand, if your market size is limited (say Fortune 100 Retailers) or heterogeneous (say, across Retail, Pharma, Airlines, etc.), the call is more subjective.

I've worked in enterprise SaaS companies that have opted not to publish any pricing publicly to give their Sales teams more ability to sell a targeted offer to their prospects. In those cases, the packages were defined internally, but there was lower price transparency which dissuaded package comparisons and enabled them to extract requisite value from prospects that had differing WTP. In this specific context, sales reps appreciated their ability to offer their prospects the right package without necessarily getting into the 'shop-a-package' discussion.

Modular Packaging

Now let's take a look at a more flexible approach to packaging that can enable us to tailor a bespoke offering to prospects.

This type of packaging can help us capture greater revenue than standardized packages that either offer more capabilities for some prospects than they need (leading to shelfware) or don't offer all capabilities needed for some prospects (leading to essentially not delivering all the value that is possible and thereby leaving money on the table).

In this case, we are not forced to come up with a universe of just three packages. In principle, this approach can lead to a high degree of permutations and combinations of features and capabilities.

Here is how to approach it:

- List down all notable features of your product and then map them to 'use cases' they enable for customers. This obviously requires a clear understanding of all the reasons for which your product is used, and thereby the product's help to solve the 'use cases' is how its value will ultimately be attributed.

- Take care to ensure the features don't overlap between use cases and that these are MECE (Mutually Exclusive Completely Exhaustive). This is important because these feature groupings that solve specific 'use cases' will become the modules at the end of the exercise, and you can't have a specific feature in two different modules.

- Once you have identified use cases and grouped features together that solve for them, the next step is to estimate the value/importance placed on these use cases across different customer segments. For e.g., enterprise customers may place a high value on security or encryption-related feature, but an SMB may not. This step then provides insights on which modules should be bundled together in a base package and which features may be added-on as ala-carte modules.

To illustrate the concept, let's look at Figure 12. In this example, we've taken a fictional CRM product that has features A through T along with a core platform infrastructure base. These features are then mapped to use cases such as 'Lead and Opportunity Management, 'Team Collaboration,' 'Marketing database,' and so on. Finally, we've estimated the value derived to different customer segments using a t-shirt sizing (M, L, XL) approach.

What does this reveal to us? Both the SMB and Enterprise segment will be well suited to have a base package bundle that includes 'Team Collaboration' and 'Lead and Opportunity Management' related features. Further, it seems like 'Sales Forecasting,' 'Sales Rep Performance Management' and 'Account Health Reporting' related features can be specific add-ons for Enterprise customers and need not be offered as options to the SMB segment. This leaves the 'Marketing Database' feature set, which can be an add-on offered to SMB customers. Now, technically we don't need to include this for Enterprise customers. But the concept of gradation still applies, and we will include it in the base package for Enterprise customers.

CRM Features	Use Case	Value for SMB	Value for Enteprise / Fortune 500
A			
B			
C	Sales forecasting	M	XL
D			
E			
F	Sales rep performance management	M	L
G			
H			
I	Account health reporting	S	XL
K			
L	Marketing database	L	M
M			
N	Team collaboration and storing signer paperwork		
O		L	L
P			
Q			
R			
S			
T	Core, e.g. Lead and Opportunity Management		
Core Platform		XL	XL

Fig. 12: Deciding on Modular Packaging Example for a SaaS CRM

The final output will look something like in Figure 13. Do note that the use case names need not be final module names. Now that we have our packaging hypothesis, we can now test this against our customer segments and see whether there is package <> segment fit and how to actually arrive at the pricing for the packages and the add-ons. That is what we cover in our next chapter.

Pro	Elite
	Add-on: Sales forecasting (A,B,C)
	Add-on: Sales rep performance management (D, E, F)
	Add-on: Account health reporting (G, H, I)
Add-on: Marketing Database (K,L)	Base Package:
Base Package:	- Lead and Opportunity Management - Team Collaboration - Marketing Database
- Lead and Opportunity Management - Team Collaboration	K L
M N O P Q R S T Core Platform	M N O P Q R S T Core Platform

Fig. 13: Finalized Modular Packaging Example for a SaaS CRM

Modularity Case in Point: Hidden Differentiators at Medallia

Price justification by packaging hidden differentiators in a monolithic enterprise software product

I've included this story to illustrate a facet of packaging that can be useful for companies selling an enterprise product, either facing a competitive challenge or a need to justify higher product ASPs. In many cases, products such as these have hidden capabilities that can creatively be brought to the fore to create a more favorable customer perception.

This story dates back to 2013 and 2014. Medallia had recently gone through a series of funding rounds and had been gaining considerable traction in the market. Medallia had always been the leader in the Customer Experience Management SaaS category and had been charging a premium price at the same time we had onboarded a brand-new sales team that was chartered with rapidly scaling Medallia's growth, which included goals around achieving even higher product ASPs (Average Selling Prices). At the same time, our value proposition and benefit statements started to look surprisingly similar to that of the competition, largely because the competition had started to adapt a lot of their value proposition to match ours. This left us with a conundrum. Prospects would ask us why we were priced so high when other vendors were making similar promises to them. While we could definitely show them our superior client roster and success stories, we were missing a crucial 'why' behind our superior product. The reason largely lay not just in the visible features of our product but a superior product architecture that allowed us (and uniquely us) to serve the needs of giant Fortune 500 organizations in a way competitors could not.

At this point, we commenced an exercise to create a marketecture (a marketing-architecture). This exercise results in a hierarchical, market-oriented representation of the Software, which breaks a monolithic product into specific modules. These modules can be given names that allude to their differentiation and value, something that wasn't apparent beforehand. Once every module within a marketecture is defined, a new sales deck is created around this functionality, capturing why it is important, what it does, how it works, and associated customer success stories.

At Medallia, one of the modules that we packaged and named distinctly was 'OrgSync.'

OrgSync was named to denote Medallia's capability in mapping highly complex and fluid organizational hierarchies into its software which could then aid user management and analytics. At some organizations, we could support as many as 70,000 users. Something that the competition could not. The act of crisply defining this module, along with differentiators and customer success stories, provided a shot in the arm of our sales team. They were better able to handle price-related objections and even put the competition on the defensive.

This example illustrates that packaging is not just an exercise of outlining which features to charge money for, but about clearly communicating the value of the product such that its value proposition becomes clear and the price is perceived to be fairly justified.

CHAPTER 4

Pricing: The Meat and Potatoes

We finally arrive at the star of the show, Pricing.

In this (long) chapter, we will first learn how to complete our initial hypothesis around packaging and pricing, where we select our pricing variable(s) and pricing structure. We will then cover research methods to test our hypothesis and refine our pricing model. Finally, we will end with considerations around our market, cost of delivery, discounting, and overall pricing intent.

Setting the Pricing Variable & Pricing Structure

Pricing Variable Selection

Selecting your key pricing variable is perhaps the most consequential decision you will make in your entire pricing and packaging exercise. If you get it right, almost every other piece of your pricing model can be fine-tuned on-the-fly. If you get it wrong, you may significantly slow down sales velocity and introduce completely unneeded friction in the sales engine.

At the end of the day, the goal for pricing is to find a way to charge your customer based on a heuristic that allows:

a) You to obtain revenue for your product that maximizes the return from the market (i.e., larger companies can pay more)

b) Your client to pay a price that is proportional to the value perceived to be derived by them.

There are many ways to think about this variable, including pricing on usage, license, seat, cost, etc.

I've found it very clarifying to look at two main approaches at the highest level as Capability and Consumption-based pricing, As mentioned by Zuora's CEO Tien Tzuo in his book **Subscribed**[9] (see Figure 14). *(The simplifying caveat here is we assume subscription-based pricing models.)*

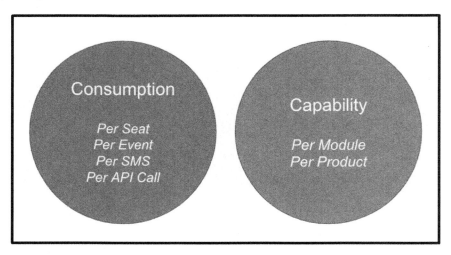

Fig. 14: Consumption and Capability-based Pricing

1. **Consumption Pricing** includes both traditional per seat-based pricing models as well as usage-based pricing models that are prevalent in newer SaaS products in the market today.

---

9 https://www.amazon.com/Subscribed-Subscription-Model-Companys-Future/dp/0525536469

- **The seat-based model is essentially a way to 'size' the client account.** The 'per seat' allows the brand to charge more from larger clients, with a sort of implicit assumption that value-derived also scales proportionately. This approach works well when the product is a more foundational 'system of record' to an organization's technology stack, such as a CRM, HR, or Customer Support system that various departments routinely use to run the business. There is unlikely to be a singular best product usage metric that aligns to the product's value for these types of products.

- **The usage-based model scales with the actual units of usage of a product.** E.g., Amplitude charges per analytics event processed, Google Drive charges on storage consumed. Twilio charges per SMS sent. Some fraud detection companies charge based on the number of transactions processed. Usage-based pricing is used for several reasons. A well selected metric can be directly tied to the value a prospect receives from the product, thereby leading to easier client adoption. It can also be useful when there are hard costs that scale with usage, think S3 storage or compute power (more often in the infrastructure layer vs. the application layer). Finally, this approach is easier to adopt when the usage of the product is actually measurable across customers.

2. **Capability Pricing** refers to pricing a product as a lump-sum amount for the capability offered. This could be a fixed price or a price that scales based on the size of the customer. Since it is a lump-sum model, this approach doesn't really allow for usage growth over time and is more akin to paying for a fixed piece of hardware or set capability. While it would definitely play well in a hardware setting, it also tends to work well for add-on modules that sit on top of a base platform that utilizes a consumption-based pricing model.

Given this information, how do you decide on your main pricing metric/variable?

Here is a proposed checklist:

1. Decide the larger model - Consumption or Capability.

2. If Capability, then the unit of pricing is per product or module, and you can move on selecting the right price point. The next section explains how to do just that.

3. If Consumption, then you need a way to decide what your key metric will actually be. Will it be a traditional per-seat model? Or will it be based on usage? If it is usage, then what is the metric of usage? I propose that you come up with a few candidates and then rank/assess them with the following list:

a) **Tie to client value:** Is the metric proportional to client value? And to what extent?

b) **Fits for clients:** Will clients perceive it to fit with the value they derive?

c) **Measurable:** Can you instrument your product so that the metric is easily measurable?

d) **Predictable:** Can clients estimate how much they will spend with this metric? If the metric isn't predictable, then clients could be hit by unexpected bills that could take them by surprise.

e) **How Costs Scale:** As your metric increases, do your costs level out, or do they scale with usage? Sometimes there may not be much choice in the matter, but this is important to note as the subsequent decisions on the pricing structure, price point, and discounting will be critical if costs increase steadily with consumption.

f) **Deal Economics:** Does this model help you create a workable sales engine? There can always be two different metrics that check all the above boxes but differ considerably in the resulting revenue and margin you accrue for each deal.

PRICE TO SCALE

Everything else being equal, you'd want to maximize revenue capture.

Now let me illustrate how this decision can have a meaningful impact with a few real-life examples:

Company	Pricing Metric Decision	Impact
Early-Stage Pricing *Helpshift*	Helpshift is a customer service software platform that originally grew due to its focus on solving mobile customer support use cases. Earlier on, the company had to make a decision on how to price its platform. Had the company used the industry-standard approach of implementing per-seat pricing, it would have significantly hampered its growth since there are not many support agents in most companies offering mobile applications, while at the same time, these apps support tens of millions of users. The company chose to price based on the number of MAU (monthly active users) and convinced the key 'Product Manager' persona that this price was justifiable and tied to value	Selling to a company with a support team of 20 agents at $100 per month would only work out to a $24,000 annual deal price. But the same company could have 20 Million MAU and be willing to pay $100 per 100,000 MAU. Leading to a monthly price of $20,000 and an annual ASP of $240,000. This was a 10x increase in revenue capture with the second pricing metric!!

	since MAU was how these products were already being managed.	
Early-Stage Pricing **Kustomer**	Kustomer is another provider in the customer service space. Unlike Helpshift, it made a decision to retain a seat-based pricing model as followed by incumbents such as Zendesk. Do note that Kustomer, in some cases, directly competed with Zendesk in the web-based support space. Kustomer's CEO, Brad Birnbaum, shared his thoughts on pricing on a Saastr podcast[10]: *"So, pricing's a really difficult thing, right? It's something that we wrestled with in the earliest days of Kustomer. We wanted to be innovative. We quickly learned as we started talking to customers that they didn't want innovative pricing. They wanted repeatable, consistent pricing that mapped to the budget they already had in place.* *Now, as we are going mid-market and above, we're*	In 2020 Facebook acquired Kustomer for $1 Billion. And while we don't have specific information on the impact on the pricing model. We do know that Kustomer was able to get a sizable chunk of mid-market customers by providing a superior product that was significantly differentiated from incumbents but within a familiar, predictable pricing model.

10 https://tomtunguz.com/should-your-startup-differentiate-on-pricing/

	mostly replacing existing solutions, whether it be Zendesk or Salesforce. So, they (customers) already had a budget in place, so they just said, "Hey, we have X amount allocated for a solution. Our solution is better, it's robust, it does more, but this is the budget that we have." *So, they wanted a pricing model that, frankly, mapped to the way they're accustomed to doing business. It was highly predictable. So, while we wanted to think about doing a consumption model here at Kustomer because we thought that was innovative, we realized our customers didn't want a consumption model."*	
Established Stage Pricing Evolution ***Mixpanel*** ***(longer case study later on in the book)***	In 2019, Mixpanel changed its key pricing metric to Monthly Tracked Users (MTUs), whereas earlier, they had used the concept of Events for a long period of their existence as an analytics software provider. They decided to change their pricing metric because the older metric of 'Events', while being	While we don't have publicly available metrics on impact, this change had a bunch of cascading benefits for the company: 1. **Reduced customer churn:** Customers were no longer saddled with paying disproportionately more compared

	very measurable, was no longer fitting with client perception of value as the company grew across use cases and industries. Some customers' usage-based bills increased substantially, but they didn't feel they received proportionate value. On the other hand, their sales team found it was hard to size up new prospects and had to do more work to translate from a prospect's actual value to the company's 'event' based pricing. They landed upon Monthly Tracked Users (MTUs) (very similar to MAUs in the last example) that checked many of the criteria I alluded to earlier: tied to value, measurable, predictable, and so on.	to the value derived. 2. **Faster sales motion:** Deals close faster as Sales don't have to play the role of translator and can keep the discussion focused on value.
Established Stage Pricing Evolution ***HubSpot***	HubSpot is a company that has come to change the field of marketing and has essentially birthed the term 'inbound marketing' around its set of marketing automation capabilities. While it initially began with a single product that was priced based on the number of contacts in	Hubspot's pricing change is too recent to know the impact, but its CFO's comment in its recent quarterly earnings report indicates that the company expects a change in its customer mix due to the pricing change.

their HubSpot instance, the company eventually made other products that weren't in congruence with being priced based on the number of contacts. In 2020, HubSpot changed its pricing metric to 'Marketing Contacts' from the original 'Contacts' metric, removing the friction that affected the company's ability to go to market with a multi-product platform.

This medium post[11] by its CTO Dharmesh Shah explains the evolution of its pricing model:

"In 2006, we were a single-product company selling what we now call Marketing Hub... Since then, we have added HubSpot CRM, Sales Hub, Service Hub, and CMS Hub to our portfolio.

...Marketing Hub was billed on a base price with included contacts, and database size — i.e., how many contacts were in the database, which we felt

In my assessment, this change would unburden the sales motion for its newer product lines and thereby both increase adoption and reduce churn for its newer product lines.

Kate Bueker A Chief Financial Officer, HubSpot, Inc[12].

"And then over the course of Q3 and Q4, what we saw is a much more balanced set of customers additions, which is what sort of leads me to the comments that from one quarter to the next, there's going to be

some difference in the kinds of customers we add, as we introduce different functionality and make pricing and packaging changes."

11 https://medium.com/swlh/marketing-contacts-pricing-lessons-38eef8301e95
12
https://ir.hubspot.com/hubfs/Q4%202020%20Earnings%20Call_Corrected%20Trans
cript_2021-02-11-20-36-05.pdf

reflected the value they got from our software.

When we transitioned into a multi-product world, the interaction between our products started creating pricing issues. HubSpot CRM is free, and Sales Hub is priced on a per-seat basis. Not only did our pricing philosophy differ across Hubs, sales activity would often generate additional contacts that would then raise the subscription price of Marketing Hub, whether or not those contacts were valuable from a marketing perspective. This created friction and confusion for customers. Our approach had not been designed for a multi-product world. As we entered a new phase of growth, it became apparent that we needed a new strategy.

When we went back to the drawing board on contact pricing...

A customer's measure of success isn't just how much they can grow their database, but how many leads in that database are worthy of nurturing. Thus, the idea of splitting

> *marketing contacts out from non-marketing contacts — and only charging customers for the contacts they needed to interact with — was born.*
>
> *Our marketing contacts pricing model allows customers to only pay for the contacts they want to market to via email or ads."*

Outside of these, you will find a lot more examples in the case study section of the book. In my personal experience, the case studies truly help illustrate the tradeoffs involved and the sizable impact of this decision. In particular, I recommend you read about how:

1. Nosto's pricing evolved from being purely usage-based initially to include capability and platform pricing elements as the company grew. I cover this in my interview with Kevin Paiser.
2. Oracle solved the problem of pricing for its marketing automation product when a part of their product saw significantly higher hard costs than other parts. This story is covered in my interview with Natalie Louie.

Once you have a hypothesis of your main pricing variable, you can move on to setting the core pricing structure.

Pricing Structure Selection

I will first discuss pricing structures for consumption-based models (which are far more complex) and then touch upon capability-based models.

At a high level, you have three options[13] to set the pricing structure for a consumption-based pricing model:

1. **Linear Model.** You charge a set unit price based on your main pricing variable, per seat, per event, etc.

2. **2-Part Tariff.** You charge a base 'platform fee' as a setup price and add the unit price. E.g., $10,000 + $0.40 per unit.

3. **3-Part Tariff.** Also known as the cell phone plan model. You offer a set number of units for a base fee and then an overage fee on top of that. E.g., 5GB of data for $40/month, $0.10 for every MB afterward (consumption model), or 100 seats for $10,000 per month and $150 per seat for every additional seat.

Here are some pros/cons that will help you select between these options:

	Pros	Cons
Linear Model	Very simple to understand and easy to tie into client value with high predictability of usage. It helps increase market penetration as it reduces risk for clients, they only pay for what they use. *(see Nosto case study)*	What you gain in the ability for higher market share, you lose in margin. This model brings in unpredictable revenue and can leave money on the table. Such a model requires accurate instrumentation to measure what a client's usage is at any time and bill them for it, thereby increasing overhead.

---

13 https://tomtunguz.com/three-part-tariffs/

2-Part Tariff	This structure will improve the linear model's revenue unpredictability while still enabling the upside of greater usage. Increasingly the most common structure. Customers are accustomed to buying software in this model and will not push back for the most part.	When this structure is implemented to drive pricing models, it can lead to 'sawtooth edges,' resulting in product pricing inconsistency. We will discuss more in this section. It neither optimizes for the highest revenue capture or highest market penetration. Depending on your intent, the other two plans might be a better fit.
3-Part Tariff	According to academic research[14], this structure maximizes revenue capture and even incents increased product usage, as long as a dominant or differentiated market player implements it. Revenue will tend to be even more predictable since the customer has committed to the highest likely usage.	This approach may not work for competitively weaker firms where buyers may be wary of over-committing spend. It requires a good fit with prospect needs. There is a chance of buyer's remorse if their needs change or didn't increase as expected. Thus, opening up downgrade or even churn conversations.

Taking this concept further, how do we think about our pricing structure for a particular plan, "Pro"?

---

14 https://res.cloudinary.com/dzawgnnlr/image/upload/q_auto/f_auto/w_auto/SSRN-id1587149.pdf

Let's do this step-by-step. First, we will create basic strawmen of the three pricing structures.

- In the linear model, we'd have a fixed $ per unit price.

- Subsequently, in the 2-Part model, we'd want to add a component of an upfront platform fee with a lower $-per-unit price. *(The $-per-unit price will naturally be lower than the linear model if we assume customers will only bear roughly the same total price for their usage)*

- Then finally, in the 3-Part model, we want to further incentivize an upfront purchase of a bunch of units such that the $-per-unit price is discounted because of the upfront purchase and the overage fee is greater to ensure the selection of the package.

The following table is a hypothetical example.

	Linear Model	2-Part Tariff	3-Part Tariff
Pro Plan	$0.40 per unit	$20,000 Platform fee + $0.30 per unit	$30,000 Platform fee with 110,000 units included + $0.30 per additional unit

Now let's visualize side-by-side the resulting revenue chart (Figure 15) obtained by deploying these three models.

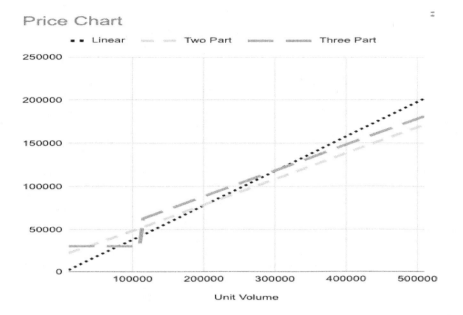

Fig. 15: Comparison of Linear, 2-Part, and 3-Part Tariff Models

The linear model certainly looks fair on a plot. In reality, the revenue is subject to consumption in any given time period, and if a customer reduces their consumption for any reason, so will your overall revenue. While this can still work for a new entrant to a market by providing no upfront fee and "pay only for what you use," bigger companies will want more predictable revenue. *(See Nosto case study later in the book).*

Now let's analyze the 2-Part and 3-Part models in relation to the linear model.

1. The 2-Part tariff model introduces a platform fee to solve the drawback of the linear model's uncertain revenue but might anchor down larger customers as the unit price increases above 200,000. Furthermore, if a customer will pay something like $150,000, then a guaranteed revenue of $20,000 does not provide revenue predictability.

2. The 3-Part tariff model can further provide a greater fixed revenue, but in its current avatar, it leads to a steep jump in price as soon as a customer enters into overages. Consequently, it works only for a sub-set of customers with lower unit volume. We really need this model to work across a wide swath of unit volume consumption.

3. Finally, in all models, we have straight lines that do not inherently offer a way to provide "volume discounts," which are expected in almost every type of consumption pricing model.

Therefore, for all three models, what we need are sub-levels (*known in industry parlance as "blocks/block pricing"*) within our models. Here is what they could look like:

Linear Model			
To	From	$/Unit Fee	
0	100,000	$0.40	
100,001	250,000	$0.35	
250,001	500,000	$0.30	

Here we introduce different pricing for different unit volume ranges, and the prices are lower at higher volume ranges as one would expect (allowing for volume-based discounts). Note that this pricing is still "pay as you go," with no platform fee included.

2-Part Model			
To	From	$/Unit Fee	Platform Fee
0	100,000	$0.30	20,000
100,001	250,000	$0.25	30,000
250,001	500,000	$0.20	40,000

We introduce similar sub-levels in the 2-Part structure and here provide lower $/unit consumption fees but introduce graded platform fees to provide revenue predictability. This is one of the most common pricing structures being used in SaaS today.

3-Part Model			
Included Units	Tier Fee	Overage $/unit	(Inferred $/unit)
100,000	35,000	$0.45	$0.35
250,000	75,000	$0.40	$0.30
500,000	125,000	$0.35	$0.25

In the 3-Part structure, we again create additional levels with higher tier/platform fees with a sizable chunk of units included in the price. Further, we keep an overage fee that is higher than the $/unit inferred fee at the top end of the units included. For example, at 100,000 units for $35,000 the inferred price is 35 cents per unit, but the overage price is 45 cents. This is done to incentivize movement into a fixed bundle, as otherwise, clients may choose to just pay as they go.

When we plot out the price chart for the models above, we see the chart in Figure 16. We now have better-looking price-volume curves with our fix that can capture increasing value for the two and three-part models as the price increases.

Note the jagged saw-tooth edges at the unit range breakpoints for both the linear and 2-part models, which is expected and is a feature of these models. When implemented in the real world, we usually try to optimize the numbers to reduce these edges, but some of the price jumps or increases at these breakpoints will remain.

Note that we can model our Two-part price curve to be very similar to the Linear model while retaining the advantages of guaranteed revenue through the platform fee. The price at every new unit volume range in the two-part model is actually the minimum price at that range, providing us more predictability overall.

Finally, the Three-part model does not suffer from the sawtooth problem at all. The price curve in this model is the lowest price possible while including overage payments such that there will be a point at which it will make more economic sense for a prospect to select a higher tier/bundle. This is what we want. It gives us even higher predictability and more revenue as per academic research.

The counter consideration to predictable revenue is client adoption. If your product is newer, clients are less likely to opt for a 3-part model and are much more likely to adopt a linear model.

It is your decision on which structure to implement. But I hope that this gives you a sense of the pros and cons involved in this decision.

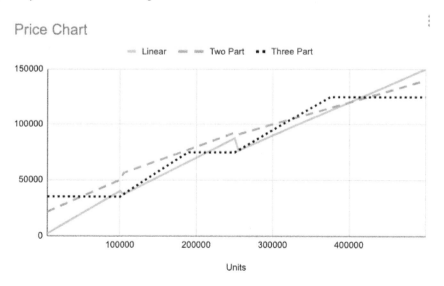

Fig. 16: Price Chart with Sub-Levels

So, where do we stand?

We have understood how to select the key pricing variable and a supporting pricing structure for a consumption-based pricing model.

Before we move on, let's take a look at capability pricing models.

Capability price is as defined, charging a set amount for a piece of software capability. A great example is Basecamp's pricing[15] at a flat $99/month independent of usage. Now I would argue that, in general, this pricing approach isn't the best for the base software since you are more likely not only to leave money on the table but actively dissuade enterprise adoption. *(The reason for the latter is best described on Tom Tunguz's blog[16])*

Where it does make a lot of sense, and where capability pricing shows up a lot is for add-on pricing. Let's say you want to add a specific piece of higher-end capability to your existing packages. Now for pricing these add-on features, you don't want to create a whole other pricing variable for consumption pricing. In my experience, it would make your sales and sales operations teams go crazy with the complexity. This is where a capability pricing approach helps (see Figure 17).

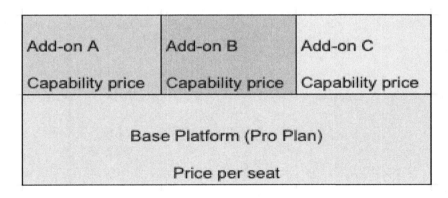

Fig 17: Add-On Capability Pricing

15 https://basecamp.com/pricing
16 https://tomtunguz.com/obscure-economic-concept-behind-saas-pricing-challenges/

Now even though it is a lump-sum amount, it still need not be a fixed price. Some add-ons can be priced as a percentage of the base fee (this enables the add-on price to scale with the size of the customer), and others can be a fixed fee (see Figure 18).

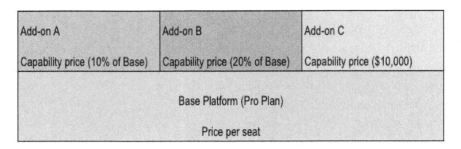

Fig. 18: Add-On Capability Pricing as Percentage of Base Price

Taking this forward, capability pricing for add-ons can be done in three ways:

Create a fixed price structure for your add-ons. For example, just say that this add-on is $5000 and call it a day. This isn't very methodical, and if this is a strategic add-on, then it limits your revenue potential for large customers, and it may even seem too expensive for small customers.

Create a % of base fee structure for your add-ons. In this case, you can say the add-on is 10% of base ACV. For our example, it would work out to $4000. This is actually better, and the price is proportional to the size of your customer. Even still, if this feature has a high cost to deliver, it may yet become cheap for smaller customers. Alternatively, for your largest customers, it could seem too expensive.

Create a % of base fee structure with a min and max. In this approach, you essentially have the benefits of option #2, with a minimum and maximum price to bound the price range to not make it too cheap or too expensive.

At this point, you should have enough information to decide on your hypothesis of a) your key pricing variable(s) and b) a pricing structure for each of your product tiers.

Testing our hypothesis & finding the right price point

So far, all we've done is built the foundations for the operations of pricing. We haven't yet determined how much to charge.

Recall our work in the previous chapter around packaging. Each of our packages caters to a specific customer segment. We will now cover how to find the right price for a given segment<>package, and the process can then be repeated across different segments.

What you end up charging for your product will be a function of the following:

1. Prospect Willingness to Pay (WTP)
2. Competitive & Category Price Points
3. Your Cost of Delivery
4. Discounting for Procurement
5. Your Pricing Strategy

Let's cover each of these, starting with the WTP of our customers/prospects.

Prospect Willingness to Pay (WTP)

Let us first start with trying to understand how to figure what our prospects will be willing to pay for our product.

Note that to understand which tactic to deploy in order to find the WTP, it is helpful to understand which one of the following two camps you fall into:

1. **You lack market feedback:** You are pricing a brand new product OR you are selling an existing product to a brand new customer segment.

2. **You have some market feedback:** You are moving from ad-hoc pricing to more scalable, predictable pricing.

When You Lack Market Feedback

If you lack market feedback, then essentially, you have two tools at your disposal to elicit your prospect's WTP.

1. You can conduct a survey in which solicit a price range feedback based on the package you've designed for the target segment.

2. You can run a conjoint analysis that will help you refine the features included in your package and the associated price point of the package.

3. You can do in-person prospect interviews. If you are selling a complex, enterprise B2B SaaS product, then you may be better served to do live customer pitch feedback sessions.

Surveys

You can use surveys to illicit a given customer's range of acceptable prices.

Let's see the example of a basic pricing survey and then the more well-known upgrade to the basic survey called the Van Westendorp Analysis. While the latter is more popular, I personally find the basic survey to be far easier to understand with clearer tradeoffs. I will explain in the following two sections.

Basic Pricing Survey

For a basic pricing survey, the two questions used to anchor responses are along the following lines:

PRICE TO SCALE

1. At what point will the product be so expensive that you would not consider buying it?
2. At what point would you think the product is priced so low that you would doubt its quality?

Note that it usually doesn't work to ask a customer how much they'd pay for a given product because the answers may get actively biased too low if the customer feels they can influence the price of the product. It is also the case that without reference points, a singular price point answer may not be very revelatory as the customer essentially is just guessing at that point.

The survey questionnaire itself should ideally be structured so that first, you can explain the context or product category you will query the customer about and then provide context on the specific product itself. By anchoring the customer in the type of solution (say CRM software), you are setting the right context of the decision. It would be fair to take through an explanation of the product with your product's purported value proposition so that the survey takers can appropriately think about the value of the product to them.

If you were to run a survey just with the two questions above to a representative population, you could then collate the results in a set of tables which follow:

Note: For conducting the survey, I would simplify the pricing structure discussed earlier into a linear $ per unit. The 2-part or 3-part tariff would simply get too complex to describe in a survey and can be eventually backed into.

Table 1

Min Price $ per Unit (e.g. Price per seat)	Percentage frequency of selection	Cumulative Percentage
20	15%	15%
30	30%	45%
40	30%	75%
50	20%	95%
60	5%	100%
70	0	100%
80	0	100%
90	0	100%
100	0	100%

Table 2

Max Price $ per Unit (e.g. Price per seat)	Percentage frequency of selection	Cumulative Percentage
20	0	0
30	0	0
40	0	0
50	10%	10%
60	20%	30%
70	20%	50%
80	25%	75%
90	10%	85%
100	15%	100%

Table 3

Price Point $ per Unit (e.g. Price per seat)	% of respondents for which price is not too low	% of respondent for which price is too high	% willing to spend the price point
20	15%	0	15%
30	45%	0	45%
40	75%	0	75%
50	95%	10%	85%
60	100%	30%	70%
70	100%	50%	50%
80	100%	75%	25%
90	100%	85%	15%
100	100%	100%	0%

Table 1 contains the frequency distribution by which respondents selected different price points being too low for the product to be of high quality. The cumulative percentage column is then helpful to find out, for how many people is a specific price not too low? In this example.

75% of people think $40 per unit is not too low of a price for this product. Table 2 essentially does the reverse of this. In the example, 50% of people think $70 per unit price is too high.

These two tables can then be combined into Table 3 to find out the % of people for which a given price is neither too low nor too high. We observe a maxima at $50 at which point 85% of people think the price is neither too low nor too high, i.e., that they would be willing to pay this price for the product. This is also called the Optimal Price Point (OPP). *(Note that the OPP is a singular price point, and that this analysis doesn't necessarily help us create a reasonable price point range, this is what the Van Westendorp approach will cover. Finally, whether or not you price at the OPP will be your personal decision taking into account costs, as well as strategic intent, i.e., optimize more market share vs. optimize for margin).*

Van Westendorp Analysis

An alternative version of the basic pricing survey is the Van Westendorp Price Sensitivity Analysis. The aim is to establish price perceptions for a product in a market. Respondents are asked four questions to determine what prices are too cheap, where a price is a bargain, when a price is high and where a price is too expensive. The crossing points obtained by plotting the cumulative curves for each of the four price questions provide four price point anchors. The resultant price "range" helps to determine the range of acceptable prices.

This can easily be done in a spreadsheet by first converting survey data in cumulative percentages, then inverting two of the question datasets, and then using the histogram function to plot the curve. This is a good article that describes this process in general: https://www.dummies.com/software/microsoft-office/excel/excel-dashboards-add-a-cumulative-percent-series-to-your-histogram/

When done, you will get a chart that looks like the one in Figure 19. It essentially shows a range of acceptable prices. The point of intersection where the same number of people think the product is Too Cheap and Not A Bargain indicates a price of marginal cheapness (PMC) - i.e., any lesser in price and a greater proportion of people will find the product to be too cheap.

The point of intersection where the same number of people think the product is <u>Too Expensive</u> and <u>Not Expensive</u> indicates a price of marginal expensiveness (PME) - i.e., any higher in price and a greater proportion of people will find the product to be too expensive—essentially giving us some reasonable bounds to play inside.

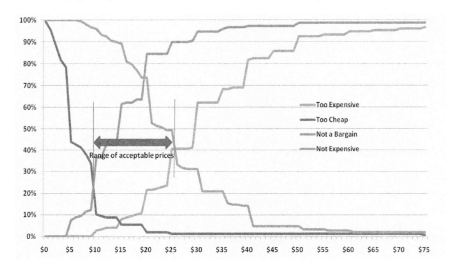

Fig. 19: Van Westendorp Analysis[17]

But this approach still has some issues. The analysis looks rigorous but is more suited for easily explainable (e.g., CPG) products where price and quality are strongly linked. This isn't always the case for software, and while the VW method gives us price ranges, they have nothing to do with competitive prices or even one's own margin. Finally, the dataset is a function of the mix of respondents at a specific point in time, so the range must be taken with a grain of salt. It should be a tool in your toolkit but realize that it provides directional guidance that should be looked at in relation to your initial hypothesis, qualitative

---

17 Source: https://www.5circles.com/van-westendorp-pricing-the-price-sensitivity-meter/

interviews, and strategic intent to arrive at the right price point for your company/product.

While the Van Westendorp analysis gives us more clarity than a simpler pricing survey, neither approach lets us estimate the relative value of different features or capabilities. To answer this, the conjoint approach offers us some more options.

Conjoint Analysis

Conjoint analysis is a powerful survey-based research technique that helps determine how people value different attributes (features, functions, and benefits) that make up an individual product or service.

The objective of conjoint analysis is to determine what combination of a limited number of attributes (for example, a tier or bundle) has the most influence on respondent choice or decision making.

A controlled set of potential products or services is shown to survey respondents, and by analyzing how they make choices among these products, the implicit valuation of the individual elements making up the product or service can be determined. These implicit valuations (*"utilities"*) can be used to create models that can help us understand how survey takers value different features or capabilities.

In the early years, conjoint analysis was applied to automobile design using a deck of conjoint cards, and the respondents sorted the supplied cards from best to worst. Based on the responses, it was possible to make deductions about the importance of "attributes" and the preference for "levels." Conjoint analysis saw good adoption in the 80s with Green and Wind publishing a case study[18] in 1989 on the use of conjoint analysis in the design of Marriott Courtyard hotels (*which I do prefer over other brands, but I digress*).

Let us look at Figure 20 to understand the basic elements of conjoint analysis.

---

18 https://pubsonline.informs.org/doi/abs/10.1287/inte.19.1.25

Attributes	Levels of each Attribute
Price	$70 per month
	$50 per month
	$30 per month
Data included	500 MB
	1 GB
	10 GB
	Unlimited
International minutes included	0 minutes
	90 minutes
	300 minutes
SMS included	300 messages
	Unlimited text

Fig. 20: Attributes and their Levels for Conjoint Analysis

Attributes are 'dimensions' of the product (brand, size, performance, price, etc.) or pricing plans (we use pricing plans in our example adapted from Conjoint.ly[19]). It is important to use attributes that, you think, drive your customers' decision-making. To arrive at this list of attributes, you may conduct a survey with a focus group and a few experts. You would also include attributes whose importance to the buying decision you really want to investigate. While the technique itself is elegant, be mindful of the customers' limitations in being able to engage with your analytical approach at a very detailed level of granularity. In general, anything more than 6-7 attributes is not advisable.

Levels are the specific values that the attribute under consideration may be assigned. These values could be real if we compare existing products or plans, or they may be proposed values if we are designing a new product or plan or want to try out newer combinations. The name

19 https://conjointly.com/guides/what-is-conjoint-analysis/

and value chosen for a Level must be understood by the respondents. Any attribute should have at least two levels if we want to consider its impact in some combination.

Once we have done the basic design of attributes and levels, we need to choose the actual combinations that we want to test out. These combinations are referred to as a Profile. Figure 21 depicts four profiles from our chosen attributes and levels. If you look back at Figure 20, you may quickly realize that all the levels and attributes can be used to generate a very large number of unique Profiles.

Since such an approach is not practical, we use some heuristics and knowledge of the industry to reduce the number of Profiles we offer to the respondents. Of course, for a complex product or plan analysis, there are more robust analytical methods available, but we do not usually get involved in that level of complex analysis. If you are of an analytical bent, I can refer you to a somewhat dated study[20] by Kuzmanovic et al., where they explain in great detail the design of conjoint analysis to study the preference of students for postpaid mobile services. There need to be at least two profiles shown to the respondent at any stage.

Attributes	Starter Plan	Voice Plan	Text Plan	Premium Plan
Price	$30 per month	$50 per month	$50 per month	$70 per month
Data included	500 MB	1 GB	10 GB	Unlimited
International minutes included	0 minutes	90 minutes	0 minutes	300 minutes
SMS included	300 messages	300 messages	Unlimited text	Unlimited text
	Choose	Choose	Choose	Choose

Fig. 21: Example of a Conjoint Task for Mobile Plan Choice

20 https://www.researchgate.net/publication/260515194_Understanding_Student_Preferences_for_Postpaid_Mobile_Services_using_Conjoint_Analysis

Figure 21 shows one "Task" given to the respondent, where they make a choice between four profiles. It is possible and often needed to present more than one task to the respondents if we need that amount of analysis. For example, we may have follow-up choice tasks for Add-Ons or Top-Ups for each of the example plans in Figure 21.

Once we have the survey results, we can obtain a quantitative measure, called a "preference score" or "partworth utility," for each attribute. Figure 22 shows an example of preference scores for attributes and levels of the mobile phone plans under consideration.

Attribute	Level	All responses
	$70 per month	-18
Price	$50 per month	0
	$30 per month	18
	500MB	-25
Data included	1GB	-10
	10GB	11
	Unlimited	23
International minutes included	0 min	-1
	90 min	-1
	300 min	2
SMS included	300 messages	-6
	Unlimited text	6

Fig. 22: Utility Scores for a Mobile Phone Plan[21]

Using the preference scores derived from the survey responses, we can simulate how the customers will express their choices for new products and concepts that do not yet exist and forecast market shares for multiple offerings in the market. We can also find out which features and pricing provide a balance between the value perceived by the customer and what it would cost to bring those to market. Figure 23 shows how different data amounts in the example mobile plan will affect a company's market share. For a more comprehensive

21 Source: https://conjointly.com/guides/what-is-conjoint-analysis/

discussion of the conjoint simulator, I will refer you to this content[22] from Sawtooth Software. You can also try out a simulation using a workbook[23] from Conjoint.ly.

While the standard conjoint analysis was based on respondents providing ratings for features or choices, the availability of automated platforms and more capable respondent devices has led to many types[24] of conjoint analysis becoming prevalent, each with its pros and cons. In practice, you can readily do enough conjoint analysis to meet your needs with workbooks you create on your own. With online surveys now par for the course, variations like Choice Based (or Discrete Choice) Conjoint (CBC), Adaptive Choice Conjoint, and Adaptive CBC (ACBC) are what you could use for bigger groups or complex analyses.

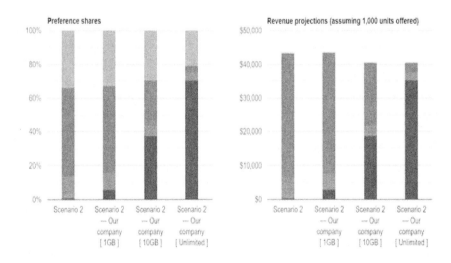

Fig. 23: Impact of Data Amount in a Mobile Plan on Market Share[25]

22 https://sawtoothsoftware.com/resources/technical-papers/introduction-to-market-simulators-for-conjoint-analysis
23 https://conjointly.com/guides/conjoint-preference-share-simulator/
24 https://www.dobney.com/Conjoint/conjoint_flavours.htm
25 https://conjointly.com/guides/what-is-conjoint-analysis/

Later in this book, you will read my interview with Jan Pasternak, who routinely uses this approach to weigh trade-offs between competing packages for SaaS products. In a webinar on the topic of pricing research methods, he shared some simplifying insights for the type of inputs and outputs we can expect from conjoint analysis and the pros and cons of the approach. I am summarizing these insights below via a fictional SaaS software example.

Figure 24 shows different package options for a fictional SaaS product and how conjoint analysis helps to understand the customer preferences/"take rate" as well as resulting revenue impact (normalized) across the packages.

Here we can see that 'Better' and 'Best' packages have more takers compared to 'Good' and 'Best+,' with 'Best' garnering the highest revenue.

Input: Package Options					
	Good	Better	Best	Best+	
Storage	5	10	Unlimited	Unlimited	
# of Active Projects	10	Unlimited	Unlimited	Unlimited	
Email Input	Not Included	Included	Included	Included	
Base Pack	Not Included	Not Included	Group	Group	None Option
Data Visualization	Not Included	Not Included	Included	Included	
Usage Reports	Not Included	Basic	Basic	Comprehensive	
Support	Business Hours	Business Hours	Business Hours	24/7	
Package Price	Free	$9	$14	$24	

Output: Take Rate & Revenue					
% Take Rate	5%	20%	25%	3%	47%
Revenue	$0	$1,800	$3,500	$720	$0

Fig. 24: Understanding Customer Preferences for a SaaS Product (credit: Jan Pasternak)

Now we cover both the pros and cons of this approach so that we understand when and when not to deploy this technique.

Pros	Cons
Relatively Inexpensive: The conjoint approach is suited for scale and is relatively inexpensive compared to in-person interviews. *(Those are covered in the next section)*	Large Sample Sizes Needed: This approach requires a high volume of responses. It can be a challenge because a typical conjoint survey will take 2-3x more time to execute than the Van Westendorp approach.
Flexible: One of the beauties of the conjoint approach is that a dataset can answer many different business questions and what-if scenarios. Even if your product team cannot deliver on a key differentiator, you can simply re-run the model with the feature removed. This saves a lot of heartache of re-doing surveys.	Mainly suited for simple products and online/web sales motion: Generally, if the packaging structure is too complex and not published on the web, then it may not be suited to be put in a conjoint survey. If you think the product needs to be explained in-person, then conjoint will not work. Customers should be able to understand the full value in a few minutes.
Accurate: Since the output of conjoint analysis is often very precise, it can help in making recommendations to your CFO.	

Qualitative Customer Research Approach

In many cases, the above-mentioned approaches of surveying methodologies may not work well for complex and/or enterprise products, as a prospect would require having a robust understanding of the product, its features, and benefits.

In such situations, we can revert to qualitative research approaches involving directly interviewing customers in one-on-one settings.

In general, we aim to interview a representative sample of our customer/market base, which can be as few as 5-10 interviews to up to 40-50 interviews depending on the size of the pricing change as well as the size of the overall business and customer base.

For each interview, we will aim to probe both open-ended feedback on product, packaging, and pricing, as well as get the customer to force rank features, benefits, and pricing options. Below I provide a suggested template[26] that you can design your own customer interview slide deck on.

Purpose	Slide
This is the first slide of the deck, meant to be a context setter for the discussion. Here is a brief snapshot of the product in question with high-level benefits and features.	Product Name: Analytics at the push of a button • Remove Blind Spots • Focus on action • Reduced cost of ownership New! New! Richer Insights and Reduced Cost of Ownership

---

26 You can download my template from here: http://bit.ly/qualitativetemplate

This second slide will then go into the goals of what we are looking for in the discussion and provide a brief agenda.

Purpose and Agenda

Purpose
- Special preview of our upcoming product release
- Understanding your needs, and fit with our new product
- Getting your inputs to refine our pricing

Agenda
- Introductions
- About you
- Product demo
- Benefits Discussion
- Roadmap
- Check-in

Depending on how you want to sequence the interview and the areas you'd like to probe, you can now start to ask questions around specific areas of interest.

Here we are forcing the client to force-rank pre-created pain point statements such that we can aggregate responses across a set of customers to validate our hypotheses. We aren't yet talking about features as

Pain Points: Force Rank

Pain Point	Rank
"It's hard for me to get to the true root cause of issues"	1
"I don't have the team to create the topics for the business units that keep asking for specific categories to track."	4
"It's hard for us to disseminate Text Analytics insights throughout the organization"	2
"I don't have full flexibility and control to manage my Text Analytics program."	3
"I'm not sure if I'm capturing all the topics that my customers are talking about."	5
"No accountability for end users to read the verbatim and take action."	6

the client doesn't understand the product yet.	
The same question from the last slide can also be asked by making customers distribute $100 amongst the areas of pain. This may provide a further level of granularity if two or three choices are perceived to be of similar weights.	**Pain Points: Distribute $100** "It's hard for me to get to the true root cause of issues" — 40 "I don't have the team to create the topics for the business units that keep asking for specific categories to track." — 10 "It's hard for us to disseminate Text Analytics insights throughout the organization" — 35 "I don't have full flexibility and control to manage my Text Analytics program." — 15 "I'm not sure if I'm capturing all the topics that my customers are talking about." — 0 "No accountability for end users to read the verbatim and take action." — 0
At this point, we can proceed to do a 15-20 minute demo of the product and the main features we want the customer to understand. Make sure the demo clarifies to the customer exactly what the product and features do.	**Demo**

This slide right after the demo is to capture open-ended feedback right after the demo. Often it can bring out areas of opportunity or peculiar objection that you may not have anticipated.

Thoughts & Reactions

Open Ended Feedback

Now that the customer understands the product, you can do a similar structured analysis on product benefits.

Benefits: Force Rank

Pain Point	Rank
Reduced total cost of ownership	1
Going faster from insight to action	4
No more blind spots	2
Moving from configuration to strategic analysis	3
Anything you'd add?	5

What resonates?

A higher granularity benefits analysis.

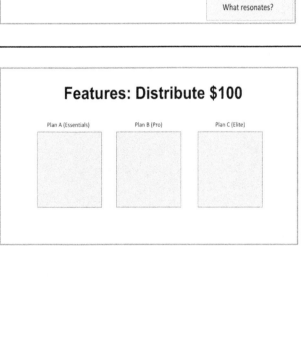

The same approach to analysis is now extended to different options of packaging. In this slide the customer is asked to distribute $100 amongst the Essential, Pro, and Elite package to identify what seems to be the best fit.

Continuing this analysis, for the package in which the customer assigns the highest value, you can isolate the most important and least important feature for the customer to understand which features drive the most value.

Features: Force Choice

Plan B (Pro)

1. What feature can you not live without?

2. If we dropped one feature - which one would have no impact to you at all?

Now you can move into getting customer opinions on the best pricing metric. Is a per-seat model more favorable, or is a usage-based model better? This is very important, as we've discussed earlier, since the proper selection of the pricing metric can be significantly impactful.

Pricing Structure

Consumption Model		Capability Model
Price per use	OR	Price per seat/user
2 Part Tariff	OR	3 Part Tariff

Having asked questions about structure, you can then go into asking pricing survey-type questions to converge on a reasonable price band based on the preferred price metric.	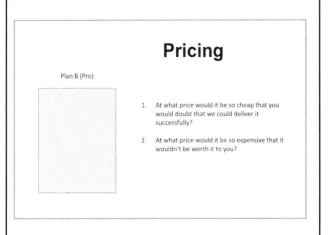
Having gone through the questions around positioning, packaging, and pricing, the other area you can probe is product direction. Here we give the customers a list of features that we are considering building and force them to choose the two most important out of four provided.	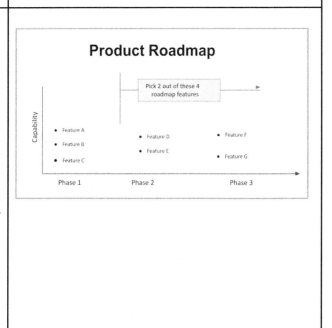

We are done with our detailed questions, and now is the time to check-in and see if the customer would buy. Here we probe a bit more on whether this seems like a fit, urgency of purchase, perceived differentiation, and budgetary decisions. Often, we can get favorable answers on positioning and pricing, but when probed to think about actually purchasing the product, a customer might have 2-3 other higher priority items. This slide will help us understand our offering is compelling for the customer.

Final Check-in

1. **Fit:** How does this fit for you?
2. **Budget:** How would you justify it?
3. **Differentiation:** What do you see as unique from other solutions?
4. **Urgency:** Where does this rank on your to-do list?
5. **Overall:** Grade?

The Post-Interview Debrief

After each customer interview, the interviewer or interviewing team then does a self-assessment to rate (on a 0-to-10 scale) the customer's fit with the product and/or package as well as rate the customer on their willingness to buy (0-to-10). In addition to the data collected during the interview process, these ratings will help us judge how close we are to this being a viable, revenue-generating product offering.

Tabulating the feedback

After having gone through this process across our sample set of customers, we will compile the data in a spreadsheet that can then be used for further analysis. It will also be helpful to add other firmographic data such as revenue or employee size to the sheet that will help put the data in context.

The screenshot below shows one way to organize this data.

	Company A	Company B	Company C	Company D	Company E
Top Pain Point	Option a	Option a	Option b	Option b	Option a
Top Ranked Feature	a	a	b	c	a
Top Package	Essentials	Pro	Pro	Elite	Elite
Preferred Pricing Metric	Pay per event	Pay per event	Pay per event	Pay per event	Pay per event
Price below which too cheap ($/event)	0.25	0.33	0.45	0.5	0.45
Price above which too expensive ($/event)	1	2	2.5	2.5	3
Product Fit	5	7	8	8	9
Willingness to Buy	4	8	7	10	10
Revenue	$5M	$20M	$30M	$200M	$350M

Analysis

Now that we have our data prepped, we can analyze the data to answer some key questions: What are the most pertinent pain points? Which customer segments do we have the best fit with? Does our packaging align with our customer segments? What is the most preferred pricing metric?

While a lot of the analysis will be simple, I would like to stress on the chart in Figure 25 that provides a strategic assessment of our product-market fit (based on our self-assessment). When combined with firmographic data, in this case, we can observe that larger revenue companies in this example tend to have a better fit with our product. Based on this, we can decide to revise our ICP (Ideal customer profile) and even avoid going after smaller companies where the fit may not be so good, thereby helping create a stronger sales motion.

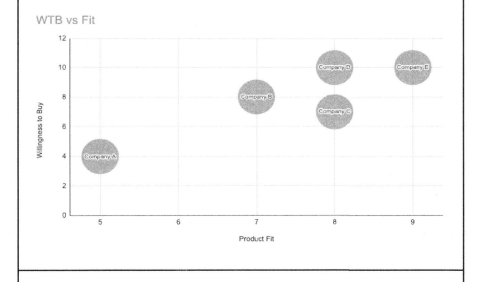

Fig. 25: Discovered Product-Market Fit

When You Have Market Feedback

If you have had somewhat of a functional, running sales motion, you may already have empirical data on how much different customers are willing to pay for your product. The first thing to do would be to make a list of all existing customers, the price at which their account was sold, and the driving unit price metrics (e.g., employees or usage volume). Then rank order this list such that you can plot a chart that looks something like the one in Figure 26. *(This exercise can be done for either your entire customer base or just for a given tier/package)*

What we are trying to understand is:

- How much does the market really bear for this product?
- How much are we discounting?
- And can we identify customer segments by looking at the data that might have more WTP than others?

In this hypothetical example, we assume our company has sold 10 customers so far on the product we are trying to price. We can further label clients based on their consumed unit volume of our product *(assuming that was our key pricing metric)*

Fig. 26: Understanding Your Customer Using Existing Pricing Data

What does the data show?

We can see that Large customers tend to pay 2-10x more than Small customers. In this chart, we can see that in some cases, the company is selling at prices higher than the list price, i.e., negative discounting. We can also see that list prices are 30% to 50% higher than actual per account ARR for Large customers.

In general, in B2B software, one can expect commercial (i.e., smaller) deal discounting to be up to 20%, and for enterprise (i.e., your larger customers) deal discounting to be up to 80%. Here we can clearly see that we likely need to increase list prices to get into a positive discounting range for smaller deals, and while discounting for larger customers seems to be in line.

Another instructive chart to look at for the same data set is to look at unit pricing, i.e., ACV divided by unit volume. In the chart in Figure 27, we can see a reduction in unit price as deal sizes become bigger. Larger customers pay around $0.60 per unit, but smaller customers pay around $2.10 per unit. This is perfectly acceptable in SaaS pricing as customers expect to get a 'volume discount' if they are using more of the service or buying more licenses/seats, etc. What this does help us with is give us our current 'price points' across different segments. If our sales motion was largely priced ad-hoc, now we have more data around which price points our packages will need to be close to in order to work. However, if you plan to change your key pricing variable, pricing structure or introduce new customer segments, then don't make the mistake of extrapolating this data since it is derived from a sales motion with certain defining pricing assumptions and customer segments.

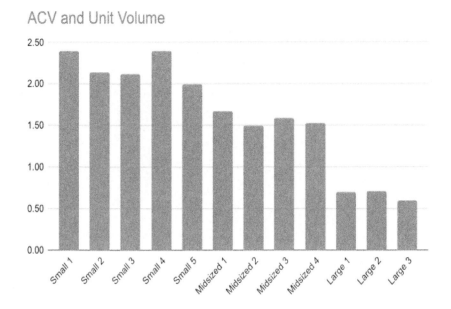

Fig. 27: Unit Prices Versus Deal Size

While the charts in Figures 26 and 27 helped more in understanding the price point across segments, we can also do analysis to help validate our packaging approach. We can now pick 5-7 critical features and see how the usage of these features aligns with our customers.

Can we find a pattern in the data that some customers pay a unit price premium when most of the features are used? In the example in Figure 28, we can see that while all customers use feature 1 and 2, features 4 and 5 are used more often by larger customers with higher ACVs, but not at all by smaller customers. In a packaging exercise, we now know to introduce these features only to our higher-end packages.

Client	Feature 1	Feature 2	Feature 3	Feature 4	Feature 5	ACV
Small 1	x	x				12000
Small 2	x	x				15000
Small 3	x	x				17000
Small 4	x	x				18000
Small 5	x	x				16000
Midsized 1	x	x	x			25000
Midsized 2	x	x				30000
Midsized 3	x	x	x			35000
Midsized 4	x	x				32000
Large 1	x	x	x		x	70000
Large 2	x	x		x	x	100000
Large 3	x	x	x	x	x	90000

Fig. 28: Discovering the Link between Features and Unit Price Premium

Note that we are not looking to create a pricing model that fits historical data but only use historical data to get enough signals to know whether list prices should be increased or decreased and whether new packaging can be created on the basis of features that drive more value.

If, in fact, you are either changing your unit pricing variable, structure, and/or changing packages, then I would still recommend combining empirical data analysis with market/prospect research methods described in the prior section.

At this point, we have the bulk of customer feedback-based information required to finalize our packaging and pricing approach. The next sections cover some other practical areas *(such as cost of delivery, type of market, and discounting)* that need to be considered before deciding what the price will be.

About ROI: Justification vs. Price setting

There is an oft-repeated ROI-based pricing sentence I've heard over the years which goes something like "Mr. Customer, I will aim to deliver you 5x to 10x ROI and in return, I only want [1% to 10%] of the benefits accrued to you". In theory, this is an attractive approach, customers can get the majority of the value delivered, and we get a small but proportional chunk of change for our value delivered.

This is theoretically very lucrative if the value proposition was actually as strong as many companies suggest. A common mechanism by which this is demonstrated is by doing a study with an external consultant. Forrester's Total Economic Index is one such example.

Let's take a look at ROI claims across a few of these studies. Here is a sampling of what a Google search throws up when I searched for a well-known report produced by Forrester known as Total Economic Impact - TEI:

Snowflake: Forrester reveals a customer ROI of 612% and total benefits of over $21 million over three years for Snowflake's cloud data platform.

New Relic: Forrester's interview with an existing customer and subsequent financial analysis found that the interviewed organization experienced benefits of $13,277,754 over three years versus costs of $6,047,192, adding up to a net present value (NPV) of $7,230,562 and an ROI of 120%.

DataRobot: Forrester Total Economic Impact Study of DataRobot: 514% ROI and Payback within 3 Months

Snaplogic: Over a three-year period, 498% ROI $3.9 Million Benefits Present Value $3.3 Million Net Present Value ~6 Months Payback

Qualtrics: Forrester Consulting estimates the 3-year benefit of Qualtrics experience management software at $38.4 million – which is an ROI of 633%.

Twilio: $12.6 million in benefits versus costs of $3.3 million, resulting in a net present value (NPV) of $9.2 million and an ROI of 277%.

When I look at these numbers, what comes to mind is an interview I had with a CEO for a Marketing role, where he kept pushing me to explain the difference between correlation and causation.

He was miffed about a phenomenon around how marketing organizations take credit for everything a company did to be successful, where in reality, the software was just one small piece.

What's going on with these reports is something similar. On the one hand, they may not be able to isolate purely the impact of the software in question, and on the other hand, organizations cherry-pick their best customers to be used in these case studies.

Tomas Tunguz echoes this sentiment in his own blog, The Siren Song of ROI Based Pricing[27]

"If we reflect on the most successful software companies, the very largest, very few sell based on ROI. What is the return on investment of a Salesforce or a Workday deployment? How do you calculate it? How does an AE defend it?

Many times, these ROI calculations assert unquestionable numbers. <u>*But most buyers approach these kinds of arguments with skepticism and even cynicism.*</u> *Sometimes, they have been burned in the past with these kinds of arguments.*

Other times, buyers recognize that it is almost impossible to measure true return on investment. Switching costs are rarely accounted for in his calculations. Measuring increasing productivity is very difficult. Soft costs "challenge the math."

The point being that a well-paid consultant can come up with an amazing ROI number, and when your customer does this analysis at the end of the year, the numbers they see will not be this rosy. So, if you base your pricing to be a percent of ROI, you and your organization will then bear the onus of justifying it at year-end.

This is why, while all companies talk about ROI, nearly none use it for pricing.

Don't get me wrong, ROI is a great tool, but for price justification, just not for pricing.

---

27 https://tomtunguz.com/the-siren-song-of-roi-based-sales/

Competitive & Category Price Points

So far in the book, we've covered some critical elements towards setting the price of our product(s), and we've mostly looked at our value delivered to customers. Our analysis won't be complete if we don't look at the competition and the larger product segment/category we operate under.

In order to understand this, it's helpful to think about the nature of certain markets. We can broadly segment markets into the following subtypes:

1. **Blue ocean:** In this type of market, your product is replacing a different way of doing things and faces lesser head-to-head competition. Usually, this market has seen action before but now could be mistaken for a boring place to be. In this type of market, you have many more degrees of freedom on how to price and how much to price. A high WTP customer such as a national bank might end up paying 5-10x more than a national retailer. However, the issue in this market is more category, and solution evangelization and disproportionate efforts need to be made to 'get things going' in the market. Until then every sale is on its merits. Thankfully you avoid the problem of commoditization and a pressure to keep prices low.

2. **Monopolistic:** I like to call this market similar to a vacuum cleaner where one big company sucks up most of the market and sets the benchmark for product functionality and price. The customer service landscape is one such, with Zendesk taking the lion's share of market spend and attention. The CRM market is another where Salesforce sets the agenda. Smaller players exist, but only at the margins or as add-ons on top of the core functionality these players bring to the table. Head-on competitors tend to fail unless they bring a truly 10x advantage over the incumbent. Pricing in this market is in reference to the big player. If Salesforce charges $150 a seat, then your pricing is evaluated in the context of it - i.e., it becomes an anchor in the mind of prospects and customers. And if a

company pays $150/seat for its CRM, then a limited capability that adds on the CRM would automatically have to be a reasonable percentage of this price. This eventually can end up in a race to the bottom price struggle if the incumbent fails to innovate, as new players crop up and, in some cases, copy existing capabilities and offer them for cheaper.

3. **Renaissance:** I didn't have the right technical term for this market, but I call this the Renaissance market. This is a market that is being reinvigorated, and in this market a bunch of small players are vying for dominance but there isn't yet a clear leader that's emerged. The difference between this market and the Blue Ocean market is that in this market, the key package definitions and/or pricing variables (proxies for standardization in product types) start to converge amongst competitors. Value propositions are similar, but capabilities still have significant room for differentiation. There isn't much to anchor outside of the customer segment, and all focus needs to be on correctly serving your ICP. In a sense pricing agility within the right pricing structure becomes more important than having the exact right price point.

Once you understand the type of market you are in, you should have an intuitive grasp of how much you should account for competitive price points and pre-set anchors in customers' minds.

Let's now look at a few other variables before we actually come down to setting the price point.

Your Cost of Delivery

Many pricing experts and articles give some real estate to 'cost-plus pricing.' This approach essentially adds a margin amount to the cost of production of a given product. This may make sense in commoditized markets for products that have hard costs of production, but for products like software *(at least in the application layer),* it makes very little sense to do cost-plus pricing since there are mostly hard setup costs but very little production costs, or cost to serve every additional customer after that. This is also why software is generally a high-margin business. *(Some amount of cost-plus pricing may still be relevant in SaaS, and that happens the closer the software is to the infrastructure layer and tied to hard costs such as compute power, storage, etc.)*

On the whole, I am still surprised when time after time, seasoned executives push back on pricing by saying, "we need to charge more for this because it's costly to deliver," or "this x feature is really simple so why are we charging so much for it?"

For the most part, software pricing is based on perceived value to the customer and not the cost of production. Albeit there is always an implementation price charged in addition to account for the delivery of the product to the customer, but even that cannot seem unreasonable. It is reasonable for the implementation price to be 10-15% of software ACV as a benchmark in the industry today.

All that being said, costs still need to be looked at, because they can a) act to sanity-check your go-to-market strategy and b) to ensure you actually get the build-once and distribute-many economic advantage

Sanity Check Your Strategy

Let's assume it takes us $3000 to implement our software on average for a mid-sized customer (taking man-hours into account). However, you find yourself selling into a competitive SMB-focused app store environment where competitive pressure pegs down your deal sizes from $1000 to $10,000 per year. Additionally, the cost of acquisition of these customers is also SDR-driven and hence manual and could be in the $1000 to $3000 range. Now suddenly, this segment doesn't look that attractive. Not to mention the opportunity cost of focusing your reps and SDRs away from a higher ROI customer segment.

Everything about a SaaS business depends on the economics inherent to acquiring and servicing customers.

Here you come to a decision point on strategy. Do you want to take a short-term hit in this segment such that you can own more market share? This is one of the main reasons why looking at costs helps. Costs make you rethink and be sure about your strategy.

Setup vs. Ongoing Costs

As mentioned, in most cases, software has minimal ongoing costs to deliver once initially built, even taking into account cloud hosting, storage, and processing and you easily get economies of scale as you onboard more customers. This is especially true for application layer software.

However, in some instances, it doesn't quite work this way. Let's say you leverage a costly third-party solution in a consumption model yourself, upon which your service itself depends. Depending on how this cost scales with usage it may impact your margin and customer economics.

One such example is sending SMS (especially internationally), where the per SMS cost could be as high as 12cents per SMS. In this case, unless the volume of SMS sent is very low, you will have to account for this part of your capability differently than your main pricing mechanism. Not doing so would mean you end up bleeding money for customers that have a high use for this capability.

Suppose you price per seat and want to offer this capability to customers. Then just for the capability to send SMS, you want to charge this on a consumption model with its own mini pricing structure. Or you may choose to pass through these costs all together to the customers and separate out the value of your own product.

Discounting

One of the tools that can work to your advantage in B2B software pricing is discounting.

In most cases where customers negotiate the price with sales, discounting needs to be baked into the price point. This because there some default expectations of the sales process.

The advantage it has that it lets you survive without very robust statistically robust price point(s) for your product because the discounting process will automatically lead to the true price customers are willing to bear. This is the closest tool that lets us reach a price-optimized local maxima that can account for variations in WTP between customers.

As a very rough rule, you can expect discounting in different customer segments to obey the following ranges:

- Commercial: 10 to 30%
- Mid-sized: 20 to 50%
- Enterprise: 30 to 70%

Suppose you have three customer segments that can be defined by size and map to the descriptions above. In that case, you can simply pick a rough number from the ones above and essentially pad the price point you would have come up with by that amount, e.g., your commercial plans will have a buffer padding increasing the price point by 10 to 30%.

Additionally, but limiting the discounting authority of your reps, managers, and leadership in sales to steadily increasing approval limits, you actually create a sales tool for your reps that helps them build trust with their prospects as they end up fighting for a better deal for the customer. The best analogy is that you are purposely adding some friction to the sales process. Just remember, a little friction goes a long way; a lot of friction leads to a disgruntled sales team and customers who balk at the initial number they see.

Your Pricing Strategy/'Intent'

We are finally here. We've thought through positioning, packaging, our key pricing metric, pricing structure, customer/prospect WTP, and our market.

PRICE TO SCALE

The term "strategy" is much bandied about almost any relevant blog if you do a simple pricing-related Google search.

It is not used in such a high brow fashion here. This is simply a decision you make.

You have all the data around your hypothesis at hand. It is now time to take the final decision to 'set' the price points themselves. How you make this decision is up to you, and there aren't all that many approaches to this. You can price to maximize:

- **Margin**: by setting the price at the higher end of the price range which customers are willing to pay.
- **Revenue**: by balancing both the proportion of customers that will adopt your product with the price that they are willing to pay.
- **Market share**: by pricing at the lower end of the range that customers are willing to buy your product.

It is a completely unique decision for your company. You have to make the call at the end of the day.

Often companies with an enterprise-focused product may opt for maximizing margin, especially if they have a limited market size. A margin maximizing approach may even be a thought through strategy to generate viable cash flow for growing the business before pivoting the product into a mass-seller. Alternatively, a bottom-up SaaS company such as Slack or Yammer may want to shoot for maximizing market-share because their business success depends on a sort of B2B virality.

As long as you've put enough thought into your packages, pricing metric, and structure, this is a relatively easy-to-change decision. Getting the structure right at the root will always be more important than the price point.

CHAPTER 5

Don't Miss This: Expansions & Renewals

Expansions and renewals are a lever of growth that has historically been a little ignored in software GTM motions. Yet, for companies that have a strong customer base, it is a growth lever that is worth its weight in gold.

Price Intelligently includes in one of its blogs[28] that (original data from a Pacific Crest Securities SaaS Survey) on average upsells and renewals have substantially lower (up to a 4th) CAC (Customer Acquisition Costs) as compared to new customer acquisition (see Figure 28).

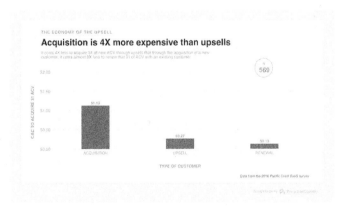

Fig. 28: Impact of Expansions and Renewals on Customer Acquisition Costs

---

28 https://www.priceintelligently.com/blog/saas-subscription-expansion-revenue-is-crucial

This point was further driven home by one of Patrick Campell's presentations[29] on the importance of monetization (see Figure 29). His research revealed that a 1% increase in monetization caused the most significant increase in profits.

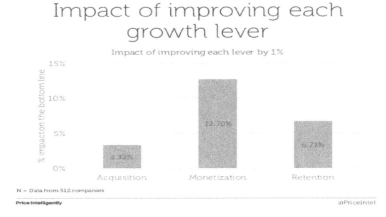

Fig. 29: Impact of Monetization on Profits

This is a critically important point for companies with an established customer base, be they single product or multi-product companies.

The problem is GTM teams (primarily Marketing and Sales) have historically not been very well structured to prospect seamlessly into existing customers, though this is changing. This is complicated by the fact that at any given time, some customers are happy, and some are not, with the Customer Success (CS) team usually gatekeeping the relationship.

In bigger organizations, there are also 'Account Manager,' i.e., "farmer," counterparts to New Business "hunters." Even so, the upsell process is by its nature different. In many cases, upsells happen as a natural consequence of increased needs as compared to a multi-channel marketing push for awareness.

---

29 https://www.priceintelligently.com/blog/monetization-matters-for-saas-growth

That being said, the point of raising this topic is to make sure it is tackled with seriousness and a different lens, given the potential impact this lever has on revenue and profit growth.

Below I provide a table of things you need to either design for or even consider as mini-projects of their own to make sure your pricing model works with expansions and renewals:

Area	Considerations
Package Design	**Caution on being too rigid** A common approach to good-better-best packaging is to bundle in all possible features within confined package tiers in the name of simplicity and deal velocity (too rigid). In some cases, this can be a mistake. If you bundle in features that have been traditionally upsold or that lie unused as shelfware once a deal is sold, you've potentially blocked downstream upsell opportunities since, going forward, new prospects will already have these features as a part of their package. *(This problem is also articulated by Johnny Cheng later in the book and borne out by his experience at Gainsight).* **Treat existing customers as special** Often applying the same rules to existing customers as new customers can result in difficult expansion and renewal conversations, especially if existing customers have historically been given special treatment (lower rates, more services, etc.) You may want to consider creating special upsell bundles or a granular feature menu only for current customers to buy from to ease natural, upsell transitions instead of creating all-or-

nothing propositions that current customers may shy away from.

Suppose your customer base broadly has a singular package that was sold historically, and you are now introducing graded packages. In that case, it might not make sense to make customers upgrade to the most elite tier before they can buy the add-on applicable for that tier, because in most cases the upgrade + add-on cost will preclude the upsell from even happening in the first place. This is where a special upsell feature menu might help.

Suppose your customer base is especially large in size based on annual revenue, e.g., in companies >100M ARR. In that case, you could also consider mapping customer sizes to the new graded plans and providing an incentive to move to the new plans (often a higher discount or deferred payment). If the pricing change is at a place where you are compelled to make this a companywide change with customer migrations, then it will undoubtedly become its own project and should be treated as such -- and not part of the initial pricing rollout.

Beware of cannibalization

A few types of pricing changes can introduce cannibalization risk:

Responses to commoditization, requiring companies to create premium differentiated offerings but reducing the prices for existing plans

Trying to enter down-market segment to increase market share with price-competitive plans

	Selling the same product via channel partners at heavily discounted, almost 'wholesale' prices. In each of these cases, and especially in the cases where you will publicly broadcast new packages or plans on your website, existing customers are bound to look for a better deal, thereby churning out of higher-margin plans. To avoid this fate, package design must be done very carefully, allowing for graded differentiation between existing plans and also thinking about nomenclature and service offerings differently. Customers will be less likely to want to downgrade if they think the new plan is different from what they have and that their current product + service offering is a better fit. *(Later in the book, Jan Pasternak shares some of his best practices to deal with this situation)*
Price Points	**List price conundrums** In most pricing and packaging revamps, one of the key overarching goals is often to increase product ASP (Average Selling Prices). Some new packages may be created to capture greater value, and others to capture market share. This often makes sense with the broader market in mind but can be problematic for existing customers during renewal time. Existing customers who have a substantial amount of functionality and sold on a prior package might need to upgrade to a 'premium' plan where the list price could be 2-3x higher than what they pay for their solution today. Offering customers these new plans at the new list prices may lead them to balk.

On the other hand, customers who use only lightweight features but who still pay a reasonable average unit price could be getting a much better deal with the lower-end packages created to incentivize market share. This may not go down well with leadership who thought the pricing revamp would actually increase ASPs, not reduce them.

These list price conundrums can be solved in a few different ways:

a) Providing higher discounts for existing customers
b) Creating different list prices for new packages for existing customers
c) Creating explicit, no-downgrade policies where existing customers will not be shown a lower list price than what they already pay

While option-b could be cleaner, it might be resisted by your finance team, which will want you to have consistent value for your product SKUs. The tactics deployed will be completely situation-specific.

Volume/Usage Upsell	**Contracts, instrumentation, and business process** Volume upsell is an element of pricing that is often missed in the early stages of a company's GTM. At some point, companies realize that the product usage by customers have increased multifold but that the original contract either did not have language to cap usage or charge for overages. Additionally, more often than not the product isn't

98

	instrumented properly to meter usage in the first place. Not all companies face this challenge, but many do. When revamping the pricing model, it is then critical to think about overage pricing that incentivizes clients to move into higher-value product tiers and internal mechanisms to flag an upsell motion when an account has significantly exceeded usage expectations. Furthermore, explicit language must now be put into new client and renewal contracts that make the usage clauses clear with an agreed-upon overage rate. Not having this language is bound to cause pain where every renewal opportunity becomes a challenging negotiation, increasing churn risk and forgoing potential revenue at the same time.
Cross-sells	**Incentivize clients to be loyal** It is the refrain of many single-product companies that go against behemoths such as Salesforce or Zendesk that even though they have competitive product offerings both in terms of features and price, the larger company is able to close multi-product deals by providing steep discounts to keep their clients locked into their own ecosystems. You must do that same with cross-sells. As long as an opportunity is a product fit with a client's need, it is advisable to offer special discounts and payment terms to existing clients such that it makes little sense for them to even bother running a competitive search/RFP. As a pricing leader, it may be advisable to proactively create a distinct discounting and

	approval process for cross-sells that is distinct from your new business deal closure process.

A final note on the dynamics of who your key stakeholder will be in this process. It is less likely to be the VP of Sales, and you must equally cater to the VP of Customer Success for these policies to succeed. Quoting Tom Tunguz[30]:

> "As a maturing SaaS company approaches 50% of revenue generated from renewals, customer success should rise in strategic importance to the business. After all, customer success generates half of the company's revenue. In addition, as the startup develops new products and/or capacity to expand accounts, the customer success team new bookings also become a material consideration. And the VP of CS contributes as much revenue as the VP of Sales."

---

30 https://tomtunguz.com/renewals_percent_rev/

CHAPTER 6

Pricing Example: ACME Inc's AI-powered Chatbot

The purpose of this chapter is to conduct a simulation of a pricing project using a fictitious example. The hope is to coalesce everything we've discussed so far and build a mental model for a process that you can hopefully repeatably run in your own organization.

Before we begin, let's lay down some context about our company and the product in question.

Context

In this example, we assume the role of pricing consultants to ACME Inc. ACME Inc is an established player in the Customer Experience Management domain with revenues exceeding 40Million per year. It has traditionally offered customer feedback measurement (via online surveys and call center voice analytics) technologies across a spectrum of B2C industries like Automotive, Hospitality, and Healthcare. Additionally, the market segment it tends to do well is the mid-market (revenue $10M to $1B). After a few years of significant investments into its AI capabilities, it has now launched a customer service chatbot product that it is significantly more differentiated and effective as compared to incumbent market. Our goal is now to create a packaging and pricing structure for this nascent product.

Structuring Our Project

Later in this book, I have documented two interviews that speak to the right way of structuring pricing projects, one with Jan Pasternak and the other with Joshua Bloom. I would recommend taking a look at those interviews at this stage to get some external perspectives of the process we will follow.

Whether you are an internal or external consultant, you can divide up this pricing project into the following four sections:

A. **Alignment on Goals & Process:** It is always best to have a clear discussion with the project sponsors around their goals and expectations around the impact of the project. This is also a time where you can brief them on your specific process so they understand your approach to solving this problem and have an upfront discussion on what resources you may need.

B. **Hypothesis Generation:** In this phase, we will generate our own directional hypothesis of what pricing for this new product will look like, inclusive of positioning, packaging, pricing variables, and pricing structure.

C. **Testing Our Hypothesis:** In the testing phase, we will employ both quantitative as well as primary research methods covered earlier to understand both customer and prospect feedback to our hypotheses.

D. **Iteration & Rollout:** In this final phase, we finalize the packaging and pricing based on the feedback from the testing phase and iron out the myriad elements we need to consider such that the pricing can be implemented successfully.

Alignment on Goals & Process

Expectations: Our key sponsor for this project is the VP of Product Management, and she sees this new product launch as eventually becoming a new revenue-generating key product line for the company. The company is a few years from IPO, and the company needs to demonstrate new growth levers making it an attractive investment. The VP notes that the company already sells to Operations and Support buyers, and this product could be a convenient sale into the same persona and that there are already a few beta customers lined up who have begun to use the product as a trial.

Our Assessment: With an understanding of her goals, we realize that since this is an early product launch, we will have limited empirical pricing data and need to spend some time conducting market research. On the flip side, since this is a new product, there will be limited headaches around making the new pricing and packaging work for existing clients of this product line.

In this situation, given how nascent the product is, we note that it is important for us to be directionally accurate but not extremely precise with our recommendations. It is the pricing framework that is more important to enable ACME Inc to start selling into the market faster.

Timing & Budget: We provide a rough 6-8 week estimate of project length with 2 weeks each devoted to hypothesis generation, testing, and between 2-4 weeks for rollout (depending on the amount of sales readiness needed). We also ask for a ~$10k budget for potentially conducting a WTP survey and for recruiting a pool of participants for primary research.

Hypothesis Generation

We need to generate our hypothesis around the three elements of positioning, packaging, and pricing in this phase. In the following table I list out what we question we will need to answer in this phase:

Positioning	1. What/who is the targeted ICP (ideal customer profile) and market segment for this product?
	2. What are the primary expected benefits of the product?

	3. What buyer personas are involved in the buying cycle? 4. Who are our main competitors? 5. What is our differentiation relative to the competition? 6.
Packaging	1. Given the hypothesis from positioning, what is our initial packaging proposal?
Pricing	1. What is our main pricing variable? (Consumption vs. Capability) 2. What's our initial take on pricing structure? 3. Should we display the pricing on ACME Inc's website?

To generate our hypothesis, we interview the following people:

1. The Product Manager for ACME's Chatbot *(likely to inform positioning heavily)*
2. An experienced AE who understands ACME's customers and competitors *(likely to inform packaging and pricing more)*
3. Two client Program Managers who enrolled in the beta program *(will help validate prior conversations and understand customer pain point)*

Here are the quick consolidated notes of our interviews:

(One of my repeated realizations on this topic is that a non-product management/product marketing consultant will not be able to go this deep and that good pricing and packaging is always a result of good upstream positioning. There is something invaluable to have a Product Manager/Marketer go all the way and price her product herself.)

What/who is the targeted ICP (ideal customer profile) and market segment for this product?

- This product was built with existing mid-market customers in mind. Still, the capability could also be usable by larger sized customers since the AI feature automates service issues with much greater efficiency and is suited for high case volumes found in larger organizations.

What are the primary expected benefits of the product?

- Reduction in customer support costs (human) - expecting to see a 30 to 40% reduction in agents required as compared to live chat
- Higher consumer NPS/satisfaction
- Faster issue resolution times

What buyer personas are involved in the buying cycle?

- Expect to sell to Head of Customer Support

Who are our main competitors?

- Zendesk
- Salesforce Service Cloud
- Both offer more robust customer service offerings, out of which the chatbot is one part of the solution

What is our differentiation relative to the competition?

- Much better use of AI, leading to much higher automation rates
- Competition's technology takes much longer to implement. Our product is self-service and can be built and deployed in a few days

Where are we weaker relative to the competition?

- The agent-side of our product is bare-bones and doesn't match what companies like Zendesk and Salesforce have to offer for large agent teams

Why would companies select us?

- They have a high volume of customer service requests, with relatively small teams burdened with this volume and difficulty scaling up agent counts very high
- Less complicated issues, but a high volume of customer issues
- Industries that would be a fit:
- Gaming
- Digital Media
- High Growth Tech Companies

What were the main reasons clients in the beta program were interested?

- Fast client business growth rates and high opinion of ACME Inc's current product offerings.
- Avoid extensive external RFPs

Furthermore, our AE interviewed revealed that she thinks this product could increase win-rates of ACME's main product line and that this product could be 'thrown in' to sweeten the deal. *(note that this input contradicts the VP of Product Management's intention of making this into a successful product line, so while we may not 'throw in' the product, it could be a promising upsell for certain types of clients)*

PRICE TO SCALE

We now have enough information to come up with our hypothesis on positioning, packaging, and pricing.

Positioning	Given the info provided, we can write a summary positioning statement: ACME Inc's Chatbot product <u>is</u> a purpose-built solution to automate the resolution of high-volume customer service issues <u>for</u> high growth technology-enabled companies, <u>unlike</u> (SFDC/Zendesk) ACME's proprietary AI technology can fully automate 50-60% of customer service issues and go live within days.
Packaging	Since the product is still in its nascent stage, we don't have to fret too much about packaging except for making sure we consider differing WTP between ACME's existing mid-market segment and a potential new enterprise customer segment. The packaging differentiation could simply be offering differing service levels and an option to build custom integrations that enterprise customers often need. Given this, we will create two different plans targeting mid-market and enterprise respectively, with the former being more of a self-service deployment model and the latter being a custom implementation with additional professional services support. <table><tr><td>**Pro**</td><td>**Elite**</td></tr><tr><td>The Pro package is made for clients that handle a lesser case volume per</td><td>Companies with higher case volumes would see more benefits by using</td></tr></table>

	day. Some of the features included in the Pro package are: • Base chat widget • Canned service bots • CRM integration • Tech support • Training videos	the Elite package. It is designed to be more customizable with a greater degree of support. Some of the features included in the Elite package are: • Special AI models • Custom service bots • 24x7 support • Dedicated CSM • BI analytics
Pricing	Here is where we must take a more critical decision. We could either price as the industry does, i.e., on a per-agent basis (capability model) or price based on the number of issues processed/automated (usage model). Given that the best potential fit of our product will be companies with smaller agent teams AND high customer support volume; pricing on usage would both be better tied to value and offer better revenue upside (since the alternative per agent price could limit revenue potential). In the usage-based model, we have a few options: • Price per automated (partially or fully) support case • Price per bot interaction • Price per any initiated chat/chatbot interaction	

- Price per bot step invoked

How do we decide which metric to opt for? (read Mixpanel's pricing metric case study to further dive deep into tradeoffs involved)

The metric must be a) simple to understand b) easy to track c) tied to value d) and be predictable.

While the price per automated support case might be the most directly related to the value we offer, this metric will be unpredictable as some companies will be better at building automations than others *(read a related case study on Nosto later in the book about this)*. Price per bot interaction suffers from the same problem. Pricing per bot step invoked is additionally too complex for easy understanding.

We hone in our hypothesis of the main pricing metric to be around <u>any initiated chat or chatbot interaction</u>. This selection extracts value based on usage of the product but keeps the revenue predictable as the client will still be on the hook for actually implementing the chatbots. The challenge is then to convince buyers in the sales cycle that the technology indeed performs as stated.

We are being completely cognizant that this pricing is different from the industry's established pricing model, but what enables a different metric is that the product is sufficiently differentiated.

Hypothesis Testing

Now that we have an informed hypothesis, how do we conduct a market test?

The process we follow here is roughly:

1. Identify a representative market sample
2. Select the right interview/analysis technique
3. Synthesize our learnings

To select a representative sample, we will look for high-growth technology-enabled companies within the company's customer base (this will serve as a mid-market proxy) and then get feedback from larger 'enterprise' firms from the broader market.

The number of companies we can test with depends on what methods we use, who we have access to, and our own resource constraints.

Given the newness of this product, it would be hard to get enough input on pricing from just surveys (which work well for more well-established product categories). I would expect that primary research would reveal a lot more information, and we can club that with a basic pricing range survey.

Since ACME's customer base is around 100 companies, with about 40 companies fitting the high-growth tech criteria set earlier, we should be able to get enough of a sample set from ~10 live conversations and 15-20 survey responses.

For the broader market, we will attempt to survey a few hundred enterprise companies (this will generally give us a 10-15% response rate) and do live conversations again with ~10 companies.

For primary research, we will use the template described in the earlier chapter. Specifically, our live deck will have the following sections:

- Intro to the technology/product
- Force rank pain points (relating to handling customer support issues)
- Demo
- Unprompted feedback
- Force rank benefits
- Open-ended feedback on pricing metric

- Low price (poor quality) and High price (too expensive) bounds

To test a specific price point, we would need to translate our metric to approximations that a business will understand.

Let's take the example of warbyparker.com; on checking its traffic from sitechecker.pro the total monthly visits are around 4 Million, with an average order volume of ~$150 and a 2% total conversion rate, it would work out to a monthly revenue of $12Million. Now how do we create numeric options, both for in-person interviews or surveys?

We need anchors and industry-standard assumptions.

Assuming a company such as Warbyparker spends about 10% of revenue on customer support and gets a 50-50 split in phone calls vs. online support needs, and that roughly 10% of monthly visitors need help via chat. We can estimate a total spend of $1.2 Million/month on support, $600k of which is via the online channel, from about 400,000 interactions *(assuming this will also automate any email support)*. So, their customer support spend is about $1.5 per online interaction. Now we estimate that we can reduce this number by 50%. We arrive at 75cents per interaction as the ceiling of upside we bring.

Will clients be willing to pay 10% of this? A fourth? Half?

Another way to look at this is we reduce the $600k/month number by half ~$300k/month, and as a percent of the revenue it works out to 2.5%. Can we charge .25% of revenue or .5%? These are our anchors which we will quote side-by-side with the cost per interaction.

While this can be explained in person, it will need to be posed a few different ways in a survey for us to converge on a good answer.

Here is what one of the survey questions will look like with different anchors:

Q. Below what price (cost per interaction) will you question the product's quality or effectiveness?

1. 60 cents per interaction (~*2% of revenue*)
2. 50 cents per interaction
3. 40 cents per interaction
4. 30 cents per interaction
5. 20 cents per interaction
6. 10 cents per interaction
7. 5 cents per interaction (~*0.20% of revenue*)

Here is another way to ask this question again, with different anchors.

Q. Below what price (cost per interaction) will you question the product's quality or effectiveness?

1. 60 cents per interaction (~*20% of total support costs*)
2. 50 cents per interaction
3. 40 cents per interaction
4. 30 cents per interaction
5. 20 cents per interaction
6. 10 cents per interaction
7. 5 cents per interaction (~*2% of support costs*)

Let's now assume we conduct the primary research across our two key segments. The following is an example of what aggregated feedback could look like:

Topic	Mid-market customers	Enterprise customers
Top pain points (from force rank)	• Top rank by 7/10 customers, "personnel crunch with the inability to scale	• Top rank by 8/10 customers, "customer complaints due to long phone and chat wait times."

	to demand at peak times." • Second rank by 5/10 customers, "high cost of phone support." • Third rank by 6/10 customers, "customer complaints due to long phone and chat wait times."	• Second rank by 5/10 customers, "personnel crunch with the inability to scale to demand at peak times." • Third rank by 6/10 customers, "cumbersome agent-side workflows."
Unprompted feedback on the demo	"This is cool, seems like we can offload a large chunk of our support issues to a bot." "It will help reduce our need to constantly hire." "As a tech company, we like such a seamless tech solution vs. throwing humans at the problem."	"This looks like it could mitigate customer hold times and improve NPS." "Would be a nice addition to have during peak season." "I wonder if we can also offer the automation to our agents who have to deal with clunky manual workflows in our current system."
Unprompted feedback on features within the package	"I like it. It's simple yet effective." "We might want a little bit more service available as this is a new tech for us."	"The BI capability is important for us to measure our performance. Can we equip all our managers with it?"

		"Can we build customer feedback bots to measure quality?"
Top benefits (from force rank)	<ul><li>Top rank by 8/10 customers, *"reduce personnel costs."*</li><li>Second rank by 5/10 customers, *"move to digital channels."*</li><li>Third rank by 6/10 customers, *"increase customer NPS."*</li></ul>	<ul><li>Top rank by 7/10 customers, *"increase customer NPS."*</li><li>Second rank by 6/10 customers, *"move to digital channels."*</li><li>Third rank by 5/10 customers, *"reduce personnel costs.."*</li></ul>
Open-ended feedback on pricing metric	"I think it can work as long as the price isn't exorbitant." "I like that it scales with usage. We don't like paying a large Capex type amount." "Our online analytics vendor uses a similar metric." "We pay our current vendor on a pay per seat, but I understand this is a different concept."	"The metric is fine; I hope you can discount it because our usage will be high." "We're ok with the metric as long as the product actually automates as much as you claim. A pilot will help." "We will use this with our main support solution, so it would help to only pay for when we really use it."

Price below which product will be deemed poor quality	The mode (highest frequency selection) for this question comes out to be 10 cents per interaction	The mode (highest frequency selection) for this question comes out to be 30 cents per interaction
Price above which product will be deemed too expensive	The mode (highest frequency selection) for this question comes out to be 40 cents per interaction	The mode (highest frequency selection) for this question comes out to be 70 cents per interaction

And here is a summary of the output of the WTP survey (refer to our discussion on cumulative survey tables in the prior chapter):

Mid-market				Enterprise			
Price Point Cents per interaction	% of respondents for which price is not too low	% of respondent for which price is too high	% willing to spend the price point	Price Point Cents per interaction	% of respondents for which price is not too low	% of respondent for which price is too high	% willing to spend the price point
10	15%	0	15%	10	0%	0	0%
20	55%	0	55%	20	20%	0	20%
30	85%	0	85%	30	40%	0	40%
40	95%	30%	65%	40	60%	10%	50%
50	100%	50%	50%	50	80%	25%	55%
60	100%	65%	35%	60	90%	45%	45%
70	100%	85%	15%	70	100%	75%	25%
80	100%	100%	0%	80	100%	85%	15%
90	100%	100%	0%	90	100%	100%	0%

Based on this feedback, we can surmise that the mid-market customers:

a) Care more about the cost of providing support (often because of high-cost phone channel usage and personnel required) and that customer satisfaction is important but a second priority

b)   Are more price-conscious than enterprise on price point. The highest frequency WTP (85% willing to spend) occurring at 30cents per interaction. Enterprise customers care more about customer satisfaction and NPS scores, as well as an ability to be agile to customer needs. Their highest frequency WTP (55% willing to spend) occurs at 50 cents per interaction.

c)   Do not object to the pricing metric itself.

The feedback on packages themselves is largely validating our hypothesis, with a few differences. It seems even mid-market customers may need more support, and enterprise customers asked about consumer feedback measurement.

We will now take this feedback into account into refining/defining our pricing and packaging model in the next section.

Iteration & Rollout

Finalizing Our Pricing & Packaging

Pro	Elite
We tweak this package to include more service options. • Base chat widget • Canned service bots • CRM integration • Tech support • Training videos • **Add-on**: Bundles of Service Hours	We highlight here an existing ability to measure customer feedback as a separate entity (which we will also tweak as a separate module in the product). It shows us the importance of drawing out and naming features that add value. • Special AI models • Custom bots

	• Customer Feedback bot • 24x7 support • Dedicated CSM • BI analytics
30 cents per interaction with a gradual volume discount down to 20cents per interaction. As we read in the prior chapter, we will select the 3-part tariff as it has proven to have the highest uplift in revenue. Additionally, we will set overage pricing higher than the average unit price of the main bundle to incentivize customers to move up a bundle.	60 cents per interaction with a gradual volume discount down to 40cents per interaction. As we read in the prior chapter, we will select the 3-part tariff as it has proven to have the highest uplift in revenue. Additionally, we will set overage pricing higher than the average unit price of the main bundle to incentivize customers to move up a bundle.

Pro Pricing

Included Average Monthly Interactions (x12 for year)	Price	Overage
25,000	7500	40 c

Elite Pricing

Included Average Monthly Interactions (x12 for year)	Price	Overage

50,000	13,750	35 c	25,000	15,000	70c
100,000	25,000	30 c	50,000	27,500	65c
			100,000	50,000	60c
200,000	45,000	25 c	200,000	90,000	55c
300,000	60,000	25 c	300,000	120,000	50c
And so on.			And so on.		

Operational Decisions

Should the new pricing be on the website?	This depends on the GTM model. Right now, the product is new, and we won't be dedicating a large chunk of the sales team to selling this. Hence, it might be better to show the pricing and packaging during the sales process and not on the website.

What sales collateral will we need?	We will need the following: a) A packaging grid listing out all the features per package along with constraints b) A sales deck / first call deck for the product c) An excel-based pricing calculator d) A working demo with a demo script
How do we get ops ready?	**We will need the following:** a) Making sure CRM/CPQ is updated with these 2 new SKUs b) Making sure an SOW template is ready for the product c) Ensuring verbiage around the usage limits per interaction is included in Order Forms along with language around overage rates

CHAPTER 7

Pricing Operations

We've finally done all the strategic decision-making, analysis, and internal sale to arrive at the pricing structure.

Time to celebrate? Not in the least.

Later in the book, I've documented my interview with Natalie Louie, who is currently the Sr Director of Product Marketing at Zuora. One of her quotes really resonates with my own experience of implementing a new pricing model inside a company,

> *"I would almost argue, for me at least, pricing strategy is the easy part. Pricing operations, that is where you start pulling out your hair. And that's where all you're faced with is 'no.' 'No, we can't do that.' 'No, we can't do this"*

Pricing Operations involves all systems, processes, and people involved in ensuring the new pricing model is fully adopted in your company such that the sales engine works smoothly.

Not even the best pricing model can yield any result if it's not operationalized to enable a smooth sales process and 100% adoption by the sales, professional services, ops and finance teams.

This is especially true of sales-driven cultures where ad-hoc deal-by-deal pricing has been part of a company's history.

So, let's make sure we get this right. What do we need to do?

1. **Packaging Reference Doc:** One production-ready place where your company's pricing resides such that it is always referenceable by anyone inside your company and provides complete guidance on all available features as well as constraints.
2. **Website:** Decide whether to publish your pricing and packaging on your website.
3. **Team:** Understand the different roles required to man pricing operations and then staff these roles.
4. **Pricing Calculator:** Build an easy way for your sales team to run pricing scenario analysis at the early stages of their deals.
5. **Quoting System/CPQ:** Build an easy way for your sales team to quote pricing to their prospects.
6. **Product Metering:** Decide if you need to build a metering system for the key-value metric such that you can bill customers if they are on a consumption-based model.
7. **Discounting:** Set and operationalize guardrails and rules around discounting across sales reps, sales leadership, and the CEO/CFO.

That's a lot! It really is.

Compared to the creation of the pricing model, the implementation takes 3-5x the amount of effort (depending on which items you check off this list above). I say this to caution you before committing a full implementation in 4-6 weeks (*been there, done that*) and that any meaningful rollout will take at least a quarter (3 months), often more.

With that caution out of the way, let's now discuss each of these items.

Packaging Grid

One document that will help align your packaging with all GTM stakeholders internally (product, sales, sales engineering, finance, you name it) is a simple shared (and up-to-date) product packaging grid that lists out the features included in each Tier.

The following table below shows a simplified version of such a grid. The effort taken to keep the document current (mostly once-a-quarter updates) is always well worth it in having clarity about basic questions, 'what can we sell?', 'what's in the elite plan?', 'does this work in Europe?', 'how complex is the integration?' and so on.

Once in place, this will help in a number of ways: It can help provide answers for RFP questions, serve as a source of truth internally and limit one-off questions on a feature or package set *(of which there will be plenty once a new pricing model is released).*

Product	Customer Facing Feature Name	Pro	Elite	Constraints	AMER	UK / EU	Need to know about implementation
Product A	Widget A	TRUE	TRUE		Avail	Avail	
	Widget B	TRUE	TRUE		Avail	NA	
	Widget C		TRUE		Avail	Avail	
	Widget D		TRUE	Does not work in EU	Avail	Avail	
	Add-on: Feature X	TRUE	TRUE		Avail	Avail	Requires special integration, delaying implementation
	Add-on: Feature Y		TRUE		Avail	NA	
	Add-on: Feature Z		TRUE	Does not work in EU	Avail	Avail	

Website Pricing Page

The decision to publish pricing on your website should not be taken lightly, and it should align with your overall GTM strategy.

There is today a consensus within SaaS circles that publishing your pricing is a de-facto good thing -- on this point, I disagree. This is a decision that requires thought.

Publishing pricing on the website makes more sense for high-velocity sales engines with a more transactional sale and cut and dry packages, but less so when the deals are complex, low velocity with larger deal sizes. As soon as you publish your pricing on the website, it forces you to have robust differentiation between tiers as all types of customers, channel partners and even competitors will start to use this as a reference.

Publishing pricing will also lead prospects to comparison-shop and question their software needs. Existing customers may also start to want downgrades (this scenario is covered in the interview with Jan Pasternak later in the book).

Every company's GTM is different, and the decision should align with the GTM strategy. Companies who sell into:

1. Mid-market could perhaps benefit from this approach and improve selling efficiency.
2. Global 2000 and Fortune 500 firms is likely to have customers whose WTP vary widely. Publishing pricing on the website in this case may not be helpful.
3. Into both the mid-market, as well as enterprise, have a tougher decision, but as listed below they can choose to publish just the packages online and reserve the pricing to sales conversations.

What you should know is there are many options here. You can:

1. Publish your pricing and packaging in full
2. Summarize your pricing (e.g., starting from $xx,xxx with yyy units included) and packaging but leave complex questions to sales calls
3. Publish a summary of your packages and leave pricing discussions to sales
4. Reorient the pricing page to communicate value proposition and use it as a lead source
5.

There are thousands of examples of pricing pages out there. Let's consider a few pricing pages as mini case studies and try to analyze why a company in question may have selected to build their pricing page a certain way - a process that will guide your own thinking as you build your pricing page. Note that we may not find pricing pages for truly enterprise-facing GTM companies, so note that this discussion of analyzing publicly available pricing pages inherently suffers from an inherent self-selection bias.

Company & Page	Commentary
https://ahrefs.com/pricing 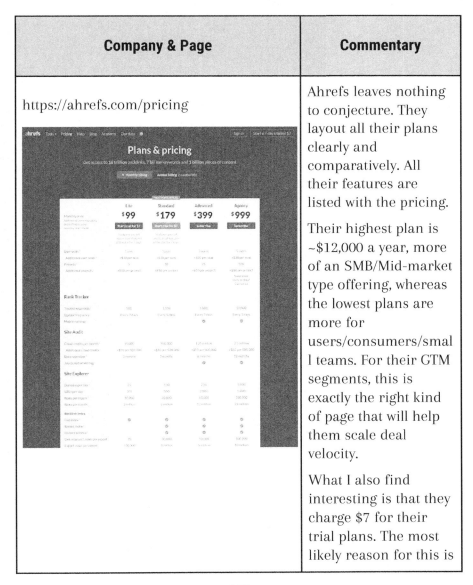	Ahrefs leaves nothing to conjecture. They layout all their plans clearly and comparatively. All their features are listed with the pricing. Their highest plan is ~$12,000 a year, more of an SMB/Mid-market type offering, whereas the lowest plans are more for users/consumers/small teams. For their GTM segments, this is exactly the right kind of page that will help them scale deal velocity. What I also find interesting is that they charge $7 for their trial plans. The most likely reason for this is

that they want to increase the trial conversion rate. Free trial conversion rates are historically really poor to convert (2-6%) and take a significant number of resources to sustain. Adding a nominal charge to use the trial weeds out non-serious users and lets the company likely achieve higher conversion rates.

https://www.aftership.com/pricing/

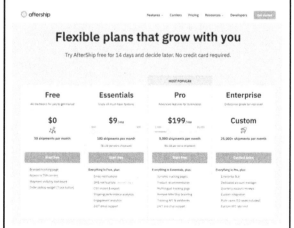

Aftership serves mostly up-and-coming D2C eCommerce brands, and thus it makes sense they keep their pricing mostly transparent.

I like their pricing page because they use the 3 Part Tariff structure that we discussed earlier with a very convenient slide scale to convert the 3 Part Tariff table into someone can easily understand visually. They display the

	overage fee in small text as well. The overage price ends up being more than the per-unit price of the tariff structure to incent customers to move up in plans, a feature of most well-designed plans.
https://www.intercom.com/pricing For Most Businesses 	I find Intercom's pricing page interesting and reflective of its size, segments, and use cases. The first sub-tab, 'For Most Businesses,' highlights primarily its product packaged into three different use cases. It is a great example of how a single product can be crafted to look as if it's built-to-purpose for a specific use case, a challenge shared by many companies that serve multiple use cases. Given the variance in use case and

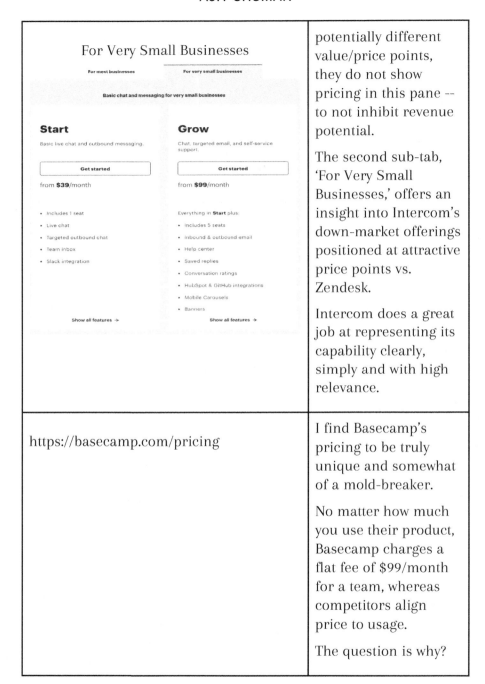

potentially different value/price points, they do not show pricing in this pane -- to not inhibit revenue potential.

The second sub-tab, 'For Very Small Businesses,' offers an insight into Intercom's down-market offerings positioned at attractive price points vs. Zendesk.

Intercom does a great job at representing its capability clearly, simply and with high relevance.

https://basecamp.com/pricing

I find Basecamp's pricing to be truly unique and somewhat of a mold-breaker.

No matter how much you use their product, Basecamp charges a flat fee of $99/month for a team, whereas competitors align price to usage.

The question is why?

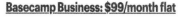

Basecamp Business: $99/month flat

If you want to run your business on Basecamp, this is the plan for you. Includes every feature we offer plus unlimited projects, unlimited users, and no per user fees.

Start a free 30 day trial
no credit card required, cancel any time

Unlimited projects
Create as many projects as you need to keep things organized.

Unlimited users
Invite anyone and everyone. No per seat charges.

500GB storage space
Centralize everything with loads of storage space.

Company HQ
A dedicated space to run your entire company.

Team projects
Give every team their own space to collaborate.

Unlimited clients
Work with clients & contractors in Basecamp.

Advanced client access
Gain total control over what clients can see.

Project templates
Save time by rapidly spinning up similar projects.

Priority support
Jump to the front of the line when you need help.

Save big with Basecamp.

Basecamp replaces a bunch of apps. See how our all-in-one, fixed price compares to bundling Slack + Asana, Dropbox & Gsuite together:

Basecamp
$99/month for your team

✓ Messages
✓ Realtime chat
✓ To-do lists
✓ Schedules
✓ File storage
✓ Documents
✓ Check-ins

=
$99/month, flat.
Grow all you want, still $99/month total.

VS

Slack: realtime chat
$6.67/month per user
+
Asana Premium: to-do lists
$13.49/month per user
+
Dropbox for Teams: file storage
$15/month per user
+
Gsuite: docs, calendar
$6.00/month per user
=
$212.45/month for 5 people,
$424.90/month for 10, $1274.70 for 30...

My hypothesis for their decision is to stay an SMB/mid-market product and go to market with a purely product-led growth model.

The comparable organizations cited scale from SMB to enterprise, whereas Basecamp seems to have decided where to focus from a segment perspective.

Another hypothesis with this pricing plan is that Basecamp truly wants deep customer retention, and I would not be surprised to see their retention rates being far superior to their competitors.

Finally, if you've read about their philosophy, Basecamp has always eschewed the high-growth, high-burn Silicon Valley startup model, opting instead for a close to lifestyle business approach.

Pricing Team

In general, there are a few responsibilities that will need owners for a pricing model to be functional:

1. **Pricing Strategy:** This role involves everything that we've discussed so far in this book and includes all the work that goes into creating or revamping your company's pricing model. Additionally, this role will also need to report on the performance of the pricing model quarter over quarter to see whether it's effective, as well as interface with various stakeholders within a company who have feedback to improve the model. On a day-to-day basis, this function will also be often on the phone with a sales rep acting as a pricing consultant and helping her/him close their deals *(super important)*. This is often headed by the Marketing team, which works in collaboration with multiple departments and with the sponsorship of the CEO or COO.

2. **Pricing Ops:** This is another heavy-duty and distinct function. It involves creating the processes and system that take the on-paper pricing model and operationalize it. It involves implementing a CPQ system (if relevant), interfacing with the finance department, understanding how clients will be billed as well as interfacing with legal to ensure a smooth sales motion. Outside of known problems to work on such as the CPQ system, the biggest issue this function needs to define in collaboration with the Pricing Strategy function is around processes - does new pricing change the expansion/renewal motion? How will overages be billed in a consumption model? What system will sync customer usage? What process needs to be built around pricing new features, experimental features, etc.? Who gets to discount and by how much? How will internal approval processes for discounts or non-standard features work? This function is headed by the Sales Operations or the Revenue Operations team.

3. **Deal Desk:** This in my opinion is the "last mile" function that stands between you and a successful pricing model rollout. If run properly, this function ensures the latest price book is used by sales and there is both a fast turnaround to sales' requests as well as a check on what sales can get away with. This function is also often part of the Sales Operations org but can also reside in Finance.

Pricing Calculator

In most organizations, building out a simple pricing calculator in Excel or Google Docs can be a very powerful enablement tool, and not just for sales but also for folks in your product team, sales operations team, finance and more.

Now let me couch the word 'simple.' It is only simple in relation to a CPQ build-out but can be significantly involved. When I've previously created a calculator based on new packaging and pricing it took me well over 2-3 weeks to cover all our pricing scenarios. I built it in a user friendly way such that sales reps could easily duplicate the main tab of the calculator and get cracking at pricing.

Often you will need to build out both CPQ and a Pricing Calculator, with the former being more of a gold standard quoting system and the latter being an agile sales and productivity tool.

Figure 30 illustrates a (fairly) simplified representation of a google-doc based calculator.

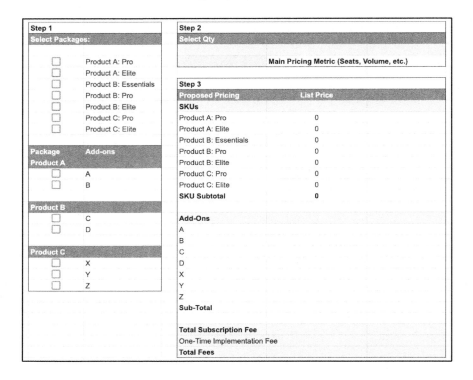

Fig. 30: A Simple Pricing Calculator

The simple calculator depiction shows that to price out a certain package, a sales rep needs only to take three simple steps to get to the price. Check off the packages and add-ons in question, enter the estimated quantity of the main pricing variable and then note the itemized price for their selection.

In most cases this can be really useful to provide a price range to prospects in the initial stages of a deal, followed later by using CPQ to formalize the process.

In reality, the calculator won't be so simple. You will likely have many more SKUs, add-ons and special conditions to abide by. Even so, I hope this provides a general idea of what the inputs and outputs should look like.

The internet will probably give you dozens of such examples, but here just a few things to note:

1. **Make the calculator super simple to use:** I'd be thousands of dollars richer if I had a buck for every time a sales rep wanted me to price out their deal for a specific situation. Even if your formulae are complex, the UI should be super simple to use for your sales reps.

2. **Realize that it's a piece of software:** As soon as you release a version of the calculator, you will start to get a lot of usage and your pricing or packaging may have small changes or errors caught as things proceed. You'll need to set it up such that all your reps can always access the latest version of this software. Do not open up a single tab for everyone to use, do not commit to fixing every rep's version either. The best process is to keep either a protected google sheet or a tab that the reps cannot modify but can be routinely copied for pricing work. When you release an update, you will have to combine that with communication asking the reps to make new copies.

3. **Don't create long-chain formulas:** This is still related to #2, but important enough that I'm calling it out separately. Excel will let you create really intricate formulae with arcane functions - don't do it. Create simple formulae that refer to calculations from intermediate tables and sheets. Organize everything in a modular fashion because inevitably, you will change the pricing or someone else will try to modify the calculator, and if it is too complex, it will introduce unnecessary headaches. Worse still, if an executive tries to understand it and can't, they won't trust the. Keep things modular and transparent.

CPQ

Configure-Price-Quote (CPQ) refers to a system that allows a sales rep to configure a package, generate a pricing quote (*including internal approvals on discounts, etc.*) and the contractual paperwork for their deals. This enables fast deal closure while keeping a record in the CRM of what exactly was sold and for how much.

Another larger benefit is that it enables complete adherence to the pricing model. Because a software quoting implementation imposes guardrails on use cases and limitations to manually closed deals, it forces sales reps to strictly adhere to the pricing model deployed. Quoting Johnny Cheng:

> *"My fundamental belief is that in order to do value selling, you need a lot of flexibility, a ton of flexibility. What ends up happening in a model where if you introduce a lot of flexibility, is it comes with complexity. But complexity is a deal killer; it slows down deals, complexity makes it so that the reps can't defend the deal, they can't defend the price points, they can't understand why it's at this price point. And so, in order to solve for that complexity and keep the flexibility, you have to introduce tools such as CPQ ".*

However, it is hard to implement well in practice and is something nearly every pricing leader I interviewed considers a headache or a challenge.

To implement a CPQ solution, as the pricing leader, you will need to interface with your Sales Ops, Finance and Sales teams. In most cases such an implementation should be owned by the Ops team with heavy input from you on the pricing structure.

Be warned however, that your job here starts to mimic that of a software product manager and that requirements will have to be defined fairly granularly. You will need to produce documents that cover all of the following:

- How new deals will be priced
- How upsells will be priced
- What the dependencies are between packages and add-ons
- What the discounting structure is

- Whether older pricing books should be carried over
- What is the policy is regarding grandfathering older customers
- What is the policy is regarding overages in usage
- What product data required for product usage monitoring
- What will be the process of introducing new products
- Test cases to ensure correct outputs
- Any inputs/edits on generating Order Forms or Statements of Work
- Defined approval chains for non-standard deals
- And more.

Suffice to say this work somehow always tends to take 2-3x more time than you will estimate initially, whether or not you have a consultant or an internal team building this out for you. This is so mostly because the scenarios that have to be built into this piece of software go beyond the pricing structure; they have to do with the day-to-day process (sometimes informal) of deal closure and in many cases highlights undefined policies for certain internal business processes.

Keep this timeline in mind before committing a rollout timeframe to your leadership team.

Beyond the pricing and process definition it is critical to involve some key friendly sales reps in the build phase. These reps can test to make sure the software is simple enough to use without unnecessary complexity, confusion or friction. Many implementation teams scramble to get an implementation finished without sales involvement and call it a day with a basic sales training. Inevitably this will lead to some unexpected usability or use case issues cropping up that may limit sales adoption of the product. The worst thing after months of implementation would be for your sales team to rebel, eschew the process and revert back to a totally manual way of selling — if this happens, you will be left cleaning the mess on the other hand.

There are a ton of resources online that offer best practices on CPQ implementation. One that I liked is a book on the topic, CPQ Implementation Guide by Marcin Krzych[31].

As a final note of personal opinion, fast-growing companies where pricing structure may undergo evolution every other quarter may not want to overinvest in this CPQ capability. Primarily because CPQ implementations take a long time, and by the time you have put something into product use, new requirements come up - sinking a lot of time and resources in this never-ending process. At some point you may still need to do this. I would personally live on a Google spreadsheet-based calculator until ~15-20M revenue which would provide (hopefully) enough time to have a mature internal deal closure process.

Discounting Matrix

If we've followed the considerations earlier in the book - we've built our pricing model with discounting in mind with appropriate padding in our plans. To make this usable, a very standard operational document is something called a Discounting Matrix. It lets your Sales team know the level of discounting authority different people in the team have to offer a discount to the customer.

Even if you have built say, a 40 to 50% padding in list prices, you should give your AEs lesser discounting authority than that. The idea is to include a little bit of friction in the process that lets an AE run a discount up their org hierarchy and offer something that the customer wants. Yes, it is artificial, but it works. Higher discounts must appear to your prospects as being earned or negotiated and not just given away by any sales representative.

---

31 https://www.amazon.com/CPQ-Implementation-Guide-implementing-organisation-ebook/dp/B07H64F4SM

Figure 31 presents one example of such a discounting matrix table. It shows a progressively increasing discounting and deal term authority structure across sales hierarchy levels.

Discounts & Terms	AE	VP of Sales	CFO
Platform Price	Up to 15%	Up to 30%	> 30%
Implementation	Up to 10%	Up to 15%	> 15%
Delayed Invoice	1 Month	2 Months	> 2 Months
Payment Terms	Net 15	Net 30	Net 45

Fig. 31: A Simple Discounting Matrix

Deal Desk

A strong Deal Desk partnership is critical for your pricing model to succeed in every hustle of closing deals. According to Forrester[32]:

> *"At the most basic level, the deal desk is responsible for reviewing and approving pricing and deal structure, ensuring compliance with price structure, profitability and solution components."*

Outside of your sales reps, the folks manning your Deal Desk will constantly be working with the pricing tools. They are your first line of defense in making sure the reps adhere correctly to pricing, that contracts are structured properly, that the right approvals have taken place and that the information is properly documented in your company's systems.

---

32 https://go.forrester.com/blogs/four-steps-to-a-sales-deal-desk/

Without the Deal Desk, every painstaking policy you've set around discounting, pricing or specifical approvals can be easily ignored. When the Deal Desk has organizational authority to reject processing late-stage deals which haven't followed company policies properly, it creates an incentive for reps to swim within well-defined lanes and ensure due diligence before cramming through a misfit deal. (This happens all too often in B2B enterprise software)

Given the organization, they might also be able to help you conduct an analysis on pricing performance for prior quarters.

I cannot emphasize enough how important this relationship is. You should aim to keep a weekly check-in with the Deal Desk to understand the scenarios coming up across New Business, Upsells, Cross-sells and Renewals. This meeting will undoubtedly flag to you whether the pricing model is being interpreted correctly (or not), as well as highlight rep complaints or frustrations that you can work on improving in your subsequent P&P iterations.

Pricing Analytics

Routine performance analysis on your pricing model's performance is absolutely critical for your pricing initiative to become successful. In most cases, everything from packages, pricing, and sales operations will have to be tweaked quarter over quarter for your pricing model to really work.

Here is a quick list of the metrics that I recommend measuring in a given quarter:

Average Selling Price: The product ASP is generally a board-level top-line revenue metric that offers directional information on product-line performance. The benefit of such high-level, non-granular metrics is that even across different pricing models, the ASPs can be trended over time, providing an apples-to-apples understanding of revenue movement that does not rely on knowledge of market movements or pricing model trends. Over time, it is one of the key directional indicators that investors are most interested in. Even when the underlying packaging structures change, the ASPs at the global product family level are very helpful directional indicators.

Median Selling Price: The Median Selling Price is very similar to the ASP. It would be advisable to calculate the median because if, as is usual in startups, the number of deals closed is small, then several very small or very large deals can swing the ASP. This can provide one indication as to why there is a change/swing in the ASP.

Number of Deals Closed: For the most part, for growing startups, in most quarters the number of deals closed should be slightly greater or the same than previously. In some cases, such as with COVID-19, a change in the market situation might significantly reduce the number of deals closed. In that case an increase in ASP would not mean the same thing if the number of deals closed decreased sharply. Using ASP as an indicator of how the pricing model performed helps to look at this metric to 'normalize' the true impact.

Unit Price: Just like the ASP, unit price ($ per seat or $ per unit consumption, etc.) is one of the most important factors in assessing the price power of a product or package. A gradually increasing unit price indicates how compelling prospects find your product in the market. It does better at indicating pricing power than the ASP because the ASP can often vary with a change in the deal mix (e.g., many smaller deals or many large deals), and the unit price will tend to be more stable over time.

Average volume sold: The average number of seats or estimated consumption volume sold is a metric that roughly correlates to the size of opportunities you tend to sell for a given product, segment or package. When analyzed at a package level, this will tend to be consistently different across packages as they generally tend to diverge based on the size and hence consumption need of the prospect. Two packages that aim to target different customer segments with similar average volume may indicate that you just need one package, not two.

Discounting %: Discounting is a very helpful number to analyze in the context of a given pricing model. Combined with benchmarks (both internally and for the industry), it can help inform if the price point is too low or too high. It can break internal disagreements where Sales might push for lower price points where the real discounting may not be very high. It can also be helpful to see if Sales is inflating list prices (-ve discount rates), indicating the price may be too low.

Important Segmentation Criteria: Additionally, for the above metrics to provide actionable information, the closed deal dataset you prepare would benefit from the following segmentation of data for you to truly be able to dive deeper into performance:

1. Product Family
2. Package Sold
3. Add-on Sold (if expansion)
4. Geo
5. Sales sub-team
6. Sales owner
7. Closed quarter & fiscal year
8. Other: key technical/prospect attribute

Be prepared to munge through data in excel and manually calculate these variables if the data is not readily available in your CRM (which tends to happen a lot). But the effort in analysis and understanding business performance will be worth it.

True Attribution of Pricing Model Changes

As you start this exercise, you will quickly realize that perfect attribution of the change in a pricing model is hard to measure. Given the growing nature of any business, many other factors change quarter over quarter, and say a 20-30% net change in revenue could

---

be attributed to many other variables such as new products, better market conditions, more salespeople, or better sales productivity.

The closest possible way to measure attribution would be to re-price deals sold under the new pricing model, with the older model, apply the same discounting percentages and then compare the outputs. Even then, applying the newer discounting thresholds makes it a less than perfect exercise, but it can still be helpful.

All this to say, measuring performance in practice often becomes more about whether or not the older problems experiences are solved, such as reduced ASPs, shelfware or low package adoption. If performance under the new model consistently solves these problems quarter over quarter, then that should be proof enough in most cases.

CHAPTER 8

Interviews & Case Studies with Top Pricing Leaders

The remainder of this book has a treasure trove of information hidden within interviews with the top revenue and pricing leaders in the Valley. The following table provides an easy reference on the areas covered in the interviews so that these can be read in the context of the theoretical information provided earlier in the book.

#	Interviewee	Company Discussed	Main Topic of Discussion	Concepts of Note
1	Kevin Paiser *Head of Sales at Nosto*	Nosto	Evolution of Nosto's pricing approach changed with the growth of the company.	*Main Pricing Metric* *Modular Packaging*

2	Johnny Cheng *Sr Director of Product Marketing, Coupa Software*	Gainsight	Revamping Pricing and Packaging in Mid-market and Enterprise Segments	*Structured Packaging Process* *Pricing Ops*
3	Pranav Kashyap *Head of Pricing, Mixpanel*	Mixpanel	Changing the key pricing metric to align with customer value	*Main Pricing Metric*
4	Natalie Louie *Sr Director of Product Marketing, Zuora*	Oracle	Designing pricing when parts of the product have high hard costs	*Cost Considerations* *Pricing Ops*
5	Rajeev Venkat *VP of Pricing, Verint*	Verint	Moving from perpetual licensing to a subscription model	*Packaging* *Pricing Metrics* *Enablement*
6	Joshua Bloom *Managing Partner, Simon Kucher Partners*	Simon Kucher Partners	General interview on pricing and packaging learnings	*Varied*
7	Mehul Saini, *Principal Product Marketing*	Rubrik	Moving from perpetual licensing to a	*Main Pricing Metric* *Pricing Ops*

	Manager, Rubrik		subscription model	
8	Jan Pasternak *Head of Pricing, Zoom*	Generalized	General interview on pricing and packaging learnings	*Pricing Research Methods*
9	Kevin Christian, *Director of Pricing Strategy and Operations, Infoblox*	Generalized	Pricing & Packaging for IT Infrastructure & Ops Products	*Packaging* *Pricing Metrics* *Enablement*

Kevin Paiser: An Evolving Pricing Journey at Nosto

Nosto delivers personalized shopping experiences for eCommerce brands. In this interview I spoke to Kevin Paiser, Global Head of Sales at Nosto, about multiple pricing changes he has been a part of during his tenure at Nosto:

- Moving from a pay-on-performance model to a fixed fee model.
- The evolution of packaging from being product-only to including service offerings and introducing modularity.

The content of the sections below consists of direct quotes.

Kevin on Nosto's Successive Pricing Models

I joined Nosto six years ago, and our story has been quite a roller coaster - in that the growth has been revolutionary. We make product recommendations on e-commerce websites, like those you see around Amazon. It's all about automating for a merchant and personalizing it for consumers, based in particular on their behavior on the website. We tend to be more focused on mid-market clients.

The Pay-On-Performance Model

When we started out, our go-to-market commercial strategy was on a cost-per-acquisition model. Our client would use our software and only pay on sales that we helped them generate. We got paid a percentage for everyone who clicked on a product recommendation and then converted within the same online session. To power this, we'd track events that happen on a website. If the customer ended up buying after clicking on something that was generated by our solution, we would basically charge clients a commission for that sale.

It was a great pricing model because it was ostensibly "risk-free." Clients only paid on conversions. So, we got massive product adoption — and this model helped us to really grow.

And yet, the unpredictability of how much revenue we would make - was a risk for us, as a growing business. A client could have a bad month all of a sudden, and we don't make a lot of sales because they don't. Alternatively, you have a very big peak, and you can make a lot of sales. If a client took the feature away on the website, we made no money. While being risk-free for the merchant, it was actually very risky for us.

This pay-on-performance model lasted for four or five years since the start of the company in 2013.

Transitioning to a Fixed Fee Model – The Evolution

We eventually changed into a monthly fee-fixed model by 2017-18, primarily because we expanded our product offerings. We began to realize that the newer products didn't quite fit the pay-per-click/cost-per-acquisition model and were more about consumer engagement. We needed to basically come up with a model that incentivizes clients to use more products while keeping a fair pricing model.

We did a fixed monthly fee that was set based on the revenue of the merchant. If a merchant got in $5 million on average, they would pay us based on the conversions we were getting before. We put together a rate card, saying, "Clients of X to Y revenue bands would be paying us A to B on average." A pricing table was created based on this. Then, if one more product was added (by them or us), we charged a little bit more.

A lot of vendors in our space charge a license fee as well, but that is based on site traffic levels. We decided to stick to revenue as our main value metric since it is the best measurement that gives the client a feeling that we're there to grow with them. As they grow, we do, too.

That's the main evolution we had — a fixed model to provide all products within a set plan.

Moving to Modular Packaging

We then introduced three levels of plans: Starter, Premium, and Enterprise.

Once we made this change, we saw some clients say they didn't want specific products in their plan. We packaged it basically, believing that they would adopt everything. But clients came back wanting to remove certain products and reduce the fees accordingly.

Again, we moved to modular pricing. Instead of three plans, we just kept a 'Build Your Own' plan option.

Now, when someone wants to access Nosto, they first pay a flat license fee based on revenue. Then, we ask them what modules they want, each costing X or Y based on their size.

Opening Up New Revenue Streams

In addition, we've also started charging for services. **When you do a lot of things for free at the beginning, and when you change that internally, there is massive reservation, say from the sales team.**

But when we started doing it, we realized that clients didn't question it, because they expected to pay those fees! So now, we charge fees for implementation, onboarding, and training, or other things that were previously usually done for free. This has become another good revenue stream for us.

Kevin's Thoughts on Rollout and Sales Enablement

In our initial pay-on-performance model, our pricing strategy was explained only on our website. There were no contracts signed. Once we made our initial pricing change, we began to sign contracts. We had to get educated on the process of creating contracts, negotiating on them, and the terms that people come back with when you sign 12-month contracts. A big part has also been educating sales representatives on how to handle objections because they were used to a very easy sales pitch earlier — "Use it, and if you don't make any sales, you don't pay." But the new license model change was very different.

Now with the third evolution of our pricing, we make sure that the reps are prepared. Here's how we do it:

1. We give them the rate card and ensure that they know how to use it.

2. We recommend doing test pitches and start thinking about how prospects will react. The good thing about the team is that they have a lot of questions on whether something is right or not or can be done a different way.

3. We do a lot of sessions on pricing follow-ups and make sure everyone learns it.

Putting proposals together has been another struggle — like how best to insert a nice slide that looks at the pricing proposal but does not confuse clients. At the beginning, a lot of salespeople thought they could send ahead three or four options. But clients would see too many numbers on the slide and get confused. So, we focused on making nice, presentable pricing that didn't feel chaotic and was easy for the client to comprehend.

Another thing that comes with pricing is a set of rules of engagement regarding discount approvals. There's negotiation with every client, but you also want to give some freedom for a salesperson to provide some discount levels and know-how and where to ask for certain approvals. We've had to create quite a few processes on how to do these approvals and determine who can give out the next level of discount.

Summary of Outcomes

The main shift that helped our kind of business was obviously predictability, but we've also now been able to add new products to increase our average deal size significantly. We've managed to create modules that we would have struggled to sell before. So, we've allowed our average deal size value to increase considerably and created the possibility for the Customer Success team to upsell more proactively - throughout the customer's lifetime. Finally, we've added a services revenue stream that didn't exist earlier, based on this pricing change.

Johnny Cheng: Revamping Packaging & Pricing at Gainsight

My interview with Johnny Cheng during his time at Gainsight was one of the most instructive in terms of the challenges that occur with pricing when a company is in its high growth stage. As the then Director of Product Marketing at Gainsight, Johnny commandeered Pricing Strategy, CPQ (Quote-to-Cash), Go-to-Market Pricing and Packaging, Analytics and Reporting, as well as Deal Strategy and Support. He elaborates in his own words.

<u>The content of the sections below consists of direct quotes.</u>

How Gainsight Pioneered the Customer Success Movement

Gainsight is the leader in Customer Success (CS) software. We are to CS platforms what Salesforce is for Customer Relationship Management (CRM) or what Workday is for Human Resources (HR).

The CS movement happened five or six years ago. If you look at CS roles back then, they didn't really exist in an organization. You would have a support person and an account manager — and that was basically it. Gainsight pioneered the whole CS movement and actually built a community of CS professionals — almost a set of buyers. As a consequence of the community, we started seeing elevated roles like Chief Customer Officer (CCO). Interestingly, a lot of our early adopters and champions are CCOs at a bunch of companies now.

In terms of our target buyer, it is obviously CS professionals, like the CCO and VP, who we sell to. For more traditional companies, we try to sell to IT or the Head of Support.

This is especially true for companies going through a digital transformation, moving from a perpetual license to a subscription model. Earlier, when they deployed hardware, they would just charge for support and move on. Now, as they're moving to a subscription model, they see many different customer touchpoints. And so, they need software that can basically handle that.

That's kind of our sweet spot in terms of who we sell to. We definitely have a lot of big names that really believe in this whole transformation, which takes them from what they always did to ongoing CS.

Gainsight's Pricing Challenges

One of the reasons Gainsight brought me on-board was to fix the number one thing that was broken there – pricing.

In particular, the segment that struggled the most was mid-market. Ironically, mid-market was actually their product-market fit sweet spot. Companies of that size would start to build out their Customer Success function and have the resources to automate customer interactions and workflows. So, to have a pricing model that can't help Sales monetize that demand in your target segment is bad.

In the mid-market space, at the time, Gainsight used a feature-based pricing model where it was just a good-better-best offering — that's it. You got a good-better-best package for a set price of say $1,000-$2,000-$3,000. I'll go into why that was broken.

They also had an Enterprise model, where it was just completely discrete pricing. Sales would basically make up a price. The top of the Enterprise deals worked fine with that approach because they were value selling, and they didn't need much guidance.

But Gainsight was stuck in the mid-market segment, where they didn't have the luxury of doing a return on investment (ROI) analysis of a five-year launch and building a discrete pricing model, all while wanting to sell on value and not leave money on the table.

The good-better-best model wasn't even working because they were always selling the middle-tier package each time. Even when they sold the larger tier, it was at the same Average Selling Price (ASP) as the middle tier. Not only that, but the packages created a lot of shelfware, and there were constant down sells.

Gaisight's software was extremely custom. Every company does CS differently, and every client needs their platform to be something different. It's not cookie-cutter or like Marketing Automation, with very defined for-use cases. Everyone knew how to do that. With CS, no one knew how to do it! Everyone had their own view, their own brain. The good-better-best approach didn't really work.

For larger Enterprise companies — the top ones — if you did an analysis based on their price points, it was all over the place. They were selling stuff for like $5 a user or then $1,000 a user. It was just like the Wild West. Whatever money they could get, they just went for it!

Johnny's Approach to Packaging & Pricing

Creating a Modular Packaging Solution

Looking at my past experience, one thing that worked really well was solution-based selling. We created modular solutions — think of them as Lego pieces. We could tell a salesperson, "Here are your Lego sets, you can put them together however you want." But there was a price tied to each module. It was almost like a packaged-plus-à la carte hybrid model.

In order to develop these Lego pieces, I did this packaging exercise (which I do at all of my companies) in the following steps:

1. **List out:** We broke down every single feature and just listed them all out. These usually end up in the hundreds.
2. **Group up:** Once we had these, we looked through different lenses for how to bucket these capabilities into what I call modules - capabilities that are natural to group together, like things a set of users would commonly use.
3. **Test:** When these bucketed modules were created, we started going through iterations to test them against customer segments to see whether they fit that segment's usage.

4. **Rearrange:** We also checked to confirm if the features that formed the modules were mutually exclusive and completely exhaustive (MECE) or not. Based on the testing, we broke up or combined these modules further.

5. **Categorize:** Finally, we categorized the modules we arrived at - based on their sophistication, price point, value, and a bunch of historical analyses about how they typically performed, adoption, and more.

Going through these categorizations, we started noticing patterns that helped decide packaging:

- What if these products are of very high value, they're table stakes, and used by everybody? These went into a **base package**.

- What module does only the most sophisticated customer see, is of very high value, and increases adoption? This could be its own **standalone add-on module**.

The caveat with this approach is that it requires a fine balance, and not listing out a hundred things. What you do want is to group the modules to a point where the salespeople can understand it. Then, they can sell the value of each individual one, and it can carry a discrete price.

Setting the Value Metric

The main benefit of a solution selling model is that you could have zero to two value metrics per module if you really wanted to go with that level of granularity. Our primary value metric at Gainsight was users; our secondary was number of customers.

If you think of the individual modules, they were either based on:

a) Users, or

b) Customers, or

c) Users and customers, or

d) None (which is a flat fee).

With that kind of flexibility in a model, you could start to hone in on where you really capture value. Certain things just do not make sense, aligned to users.

For example, if we had this capability that basically communicates out to customers, like marketing automation for CS. In this, you cannot just pass on the number of users — the value of this module has nothing to do with users. It has everything to do with customers, though. If I have 5,000 customers, I'm going to reach out to them and charge you based on those customers. So, certain things are measured on different levers, and what's nice is that you can tweak this on multiple axes. That was a really big change because **Gainsight, as with a lot of SaaS companies, relied too heavily on users. A lot of SaaS companies just go ahead with users as the metric, not caring if it doesn't align because they don't know how to price.**

A lot of pricing professionals aren't willing to change the value metric or explore other options because they're afraid it will mess up ASP or sales cycles. But it is one of the few things you just have to get right, even if it means tweaking it.

I learned this from my time at Marketo. When I first started there, the industry used sent email volume as the pricing metric. If you think of how that lever aligns to value — it doesn't! You can send a bunch of emails out, but it doesn't mean that you're going to capture more value from them or get more contacts. It's also extremely hard to predict how many emails you're going to send in the following year.

So, we were one of the first to pioneer the concept of pricing per contact, which actually aligns very closely to value – "If you use my product to get more leads and pay us more money, you're still more successful in return."

Finding this lever is almost like a silver bullet, which a lot of companies fail to do.

Selecting the Value Metric for 'Marketo for Mobile'

An instance of where we had the wrong lever was when we introduced Marketo for mobile — our pricing lever was the number of app downloads. We thought that since we're mobile marketing, it makes sense because the more apps your customer downloads, the better your marketing is doing, the more you pay us money. Within a month of launching pricing packaging and going out to market, we realized we had completely messed up.

If you asked any mobile-first company what metric they value, it's always monthly active users (MAUs). That's the number they put to the board and they tell investors. They don't care that they got a million people to download their apps — they want engagement. How many of those million people actually went in and touched the app? That's their MAU. We quickly pivoted as well, because when our earlier lever didn't resonate with value, we changed it up immediately.

Results of The Pricing Revamp

Impact on the Sales Process

The change was very well-received in the mid-market segment, as they now had guidance. They could do value selling. There were price curves, they understood the discount ranges, what other customers bought for, and more.

The Enterprise segment was fine with getting some structure and the discount was still up to their discretion. So, there was still a lot of value selling and proven ROI. In certain Enterprise cases, where something wasn't priced according to expectations, we would create sub-packages. These Enterprise-grade packages made it modular enough to cater to both segments.

However, with the new pricing model, where we had to be cautious of was the small to midsize (SMB) space. Here the SMB Sales reps could develop a "packaging crutch" because they didn't understand how the product/benefits tied to the customer needs– "I only sell this one package and that's all I sell. I don't care if the customer needs 20 percent of it, or more. I am just going to sell this." This way, we also didn't sell undervalue. But eventually, the company had to actually learn how to do value selling - about modules and how to position modules for customers. That was difficult, but it was a step in the right direction in terms of behavior.

Changes in Performance Metrics

A few things were really apparent:

1. Firstly, ASP obviously shot up right off the bat.
2. Annual Recurring Revenue (ARR) also went up.
3. The really good thing is we sold less for more money, which is like the Holy Grail. I sold fewer modules for more money because it felt more custom, and it was selling undervalue.
4. In return, our expansion dollars went up as well.

Overall, it was just a very positive and huge change in how we were monetizing our capabilities. This change was almost expected from me at the three companies where I headed pricing — if you make these changes and train the reps on how to use this model, the ASP will go up, and the expenses can, too.

Data Sources to Tap for Analysis & Research

The only three things I do are:

1. Talk to customers or prospects.
2. Look at historical data.
3. Look at competitive data.

I've seen a lot of McKinsey-like studies where they do a lot more, but at the end of the day, as a pricing professional, you just have to be really flexible and organic with your pricing. You can't get stuck at a figure.

You have to be able to look into analysis and optimize. **A lot of pricing professionals don't like the optimization part. It's all about just tuning, tuning, and tuning. I'm a strong believer in optimization and change my price curves, especially for newly launched products once a month. It then becomes once a quarter, then maybe once a year, and finally maybe never. But you have to keep tweaking.**

Johnny's Take on Pricing Operations: The Ups and Downs of CPQ

I have a very strong point of view on Configure, Price, and Quote (CPQ) systems. If you're just doing feature package selling, you don't really need a lot of sales tools or CPQ. It's easy enough to do, especially because it's so transparent to your customer. But once you start moving up and begin value selling, you have to start creating tools for sales. It is a must. My fundamental belief is that in order to do value selling, you need a ton of flexibility. And there is a level of complexity when you introduce it. This can be the deal killer, as it slows things down, makes it so that reps can't defend the deal or price points. It's very hard for them.

In order to address that complexity and keep the flexibility, you have to introduce tools. In every company I've been at, I'd give them both the pricing calculator and a CPQ. I'm a strong believer that the pricing calculator is used very early in a sales cycle to do budgeting, rough numbers, and packaging. CPQ is basically a guidance selling process.

Whenever I mention CPQ, a lot of people feel it is one of the worst tools to implement in the history of software. But I'm a huge fan of CPQ because it gives all that guidance and all those instruments. It also means less reliance on the Deal Desk and allows your company to scale. This is while giving you a lot of data on the backend. There are a lot of positives about CPQ, but it is painful to implement, especially if never done before.

While I led the process, it had to be in partnership with sales ops, IT, and finance — all the people actually building it. It's almost like the four legs of a table. If you're missing any of the legs, it's guaranteed that implementation will be bad, and there will be pitfalls. If your sales ops are very tuned in to sales, product, and the various spokes, things may be fine. But then, most sales ops try to build CPQ for the Deal Desk. CPQ is not a Deal Desk tool. It's a sales tool. Unless they have that perspective, it's extremely difficult.

That's why my guidance is that if you build something like a calculator in parallel with CPQ and say, "CPQ is the source of truth," the calculator basically just follows.

Pranav Kashyap: Moving to a Monthly Tracked Users Based Pricing Model at Mixpanel

Group Product Manager and Head of Pricing at Mixpanel, Pranav Kashyap, elaborates on how the company made the switch to a new pricing model.

The content of the sections below consists of direct quotes.

Why the Events Model wasn't Working

Mixpanel had an events-based pricing model initially (since 2009) until their recent change in 2019. Under the events-based model, each item that you tracked on the website was an event. This tracked very well with our costs — the more events they sent us, the more expensive it was.

The issue was that this did not work well for a lot of our customers. For one, it was really difficult for them to predict how many events they would need. Lots of people were new to the concept of tracking.

This was especially true for product analytics — it was usually Product Managers (PMs) who wanted to improve their product and see where users got stuck or how a new feature of theirs is doing, whether people were using it or not, retaining it or not. In that world, we found that if we wanted to really help our customers, the only way we could prove it was by helping them move real business metrics. That means that we had to either help them grow, or retain, or engage users more.

Events help measure some of that, but they don't always do a good job of actually tracking it. For example, if you were to track a lot of things, it might not be going well for you — but you're still paying us more money. This led to churn and dissatisfaction. For one, people would churn if their increased event volume didn't result in more revenue or usage for their company - say if they went from 10 million events to 100 million events and were still unable to find value. They were tracking more and more events and paying more money but not seeing the business benefit.

Secondly, if we asked brand new users and salespeople how many events they needed with a new account, they would not know. They knew their number of users but not how many events they needed— and that was another complication in estimating usage.

Mixpanel's Repackaging

The solution involved everything from packaging to changing the core price metric to also setting the price levels.

We first figured out which were the big customer segments and what use cases they had. We found a mix of start-ups and large customers. Within them, there were:

- **Engineering, Product and Design (EPD) teams:** At start-ups, all that the EPD teams really wanted to know was whether they were achieving product-market fit and whether they had the users that they needed. Large enterprises have lots of different teams, so they wanted to control who had access to data, who was using what, whether they had Single Sign-On (SSO), and how they were doing as a company.

- **Data teams:** Data engineering teams were very heavily involved. They wanted to connect their stack and have their data flow into Mixpanel, which was clean; or have Mixpanel data flow back into their stack.

- **·Marketing teams:** They wanted to run lots of A/B tests, do email marketing, push notifications, and so on.

These were the different groups, and each had different use cases. But certain things were consistent. Everyone wanted to know how they are doing as a company, and whether their features were being used. But then, each group had some specific nuance around that need, too.

Using all this, we repackaged Mixpanel. Earlier, we used to sell an events plan and a people plan. Then, we split it out into Mixpanel Analytics, after which you could add things on for the data team in the 'Data Pipelines Package'. For marketers, there was a 'Messaging Package'. Separately, we also had a 'Groups Package' specifically targeted at B2B companies, where we actually incurred more costs in storing data because we had to store multiple copies of it.

Pricing Research Methods Used

We ran some surveys of people to figure out what things they valued, and how much. This was to get a sense of how many dollars we should charge for the packages, what features they needed, and how we stacked up against our competition. We also did a lot of customer interviews, to try and understand what the different rules were, and what features were being used in their companies.

We didn't run any conjoint or Van Westendorp analyses. Conjoint analysis was arduous to set up and administer. It was just too granular for that, as we had almost 50-60 different features we had to plug into different places. Running a conjoint would have meant taking hour-long surveys, which can be quite hard.

Altering the Metric to Monthly Tracked Users (MTUs)

Once we had our packaging in a reasonably good place, the next thing was to change metrics. We tried lots of different metrics. We mooted charging based on how much we could improve a client's revenue growth; or we mulled basing it on monthly active users (MAUs) or monthly tracked users (MTUs).

We tested some 50 different metrics — like number of apps and websites tracked, page views, flat rates, query volume, data stored, data exported, a percentage of revenue attributed to Mixpanel, a percentage of churn reduced, and so on.

At the end of it, we managed to narrow down the list by subjecting every metric to the following five criteria33:

1. **Is it Predictable:** Customers ideally want their bills to be fairly consistent. So, do we. If there is a month-on-month variation, it is difficult for the customer to predict costs, while making it hard for us to forecast revenue. So, the question we asked was - *Can you reliably model price increases over time?* And worked to address this.

2. **Is it Acceptable to customers:** A flat rate can be a tough sell when you've got customers ranging from 10 employees to more than 100,000. We didn't want something that deterred our customers from getting the most out of our product. The idea was to see if a salesperson could sell this. We wanted to see if this seemed logical to our prospects.

3. **Is it Trackable:** With MTUs, customers know how many users they have. And we do too. That way, it is simple and straightforward for both parties.

4. **Is it Scalable:** The goal here was to strike a balance between affordability for smaller customers and volume discounts for the larger ones. We wanted to make sure that small customers who only have a budget of $100 a month could pay us alongside large customers who were paying us several million a year. The idea was to see if the model could be applied to both small companies and giant ones, and if growth could be comfortable with each.

5. **Is it aligned with value:** This was our key consideration. We ran regression analyses for every metric under consideration to see which correlated most with revenue. While Event volume didn't pass the test, it was MTUs that won by a landslide. Our philosophy was that we didn't want start-ups to pay too much. We wanted to see which of these metrics does best at keeping it

---

33 Danielle Kucera, 'Inside Mixpanel: In 2019, we realized our pricing wasn't good for our customers. Here's what we did.' https://mixpanel.com/blog/pricing-mtu-model/

cheap for a small company, by charging more for bigger companies. MTUs ended up winning on that front. It was basically how many unique people you track and served as a proxy for MAUs.

The Roll-out of the New Model

At first, it was opt-in. We already knew which customers were finding it hardest under the events model — we could analytically figure that out. We also gave the pitch to our sales team to talk to customers who were upset about the price they were paying. We did that and basically kicked off a pilot. We had salespeople go out and ask if someone would actually rather be on the new option, instead of the events pricing model. So, many customers who were initially going to churn actually liked it a lot, switched over to the new plan, and stuck around with Mixpanel.

These were all existing customers. We already had Mixpanel data on exactly how many MTUs they had — so we had a very good sense of the numbers. We found that almost everyone had Google Analytics installed on their website or their properties even for new customers.

We wanted to keep our revenues flat. So, we said, "Look, if we assume that everyone was to move over to this new plan, we want to make exactly the same money. This is not a call to make more money off our customers." Thereafter, some customers who were significantly better off with MTU would switch; and some who were significantly worse off would never switch. So, net-net we expected to lose some money as a result of the switch but hoped to make it up with churn rates - which we thought would actually decrease by 10-15 percent.

Optimizing the Model at Every Step

One learning on the sales front was that the switch made the process a lot easier. This was because the team could now figure out how much the customer needed based on Google Analytics.

What got harder was that there was more uncertainty in the model than we had realized. We're trying to get around it now but take for instance a situation in which you're tracking events on your homepage and then run a Snapchat ad that loads your homepage. Now, each person who sees that ad is pulling up your entire homepage. That blows up your MTU count because there are way more unique visitors — but they don't do anything on your product. And now that's something to pay for.

So that was an unforeseen development. We did know that some customers were very high MTU, but very few Events. To address this, we had to come up with a different pricing model called MTU Five. As part of this model, a user doesn't count as one until they've done five events. This approach tackled 90 percent of such cases.

Secondly, some things that were easier on our old model are a bit harder now. With Events (value metric), it would have been a lot easier, say if you joined on the 15th of a month and we could just count events from the 15th to the 30th for the month. With MTUs, it's harder because a month is a defined timeframe - we can only bill you on the first of every month. So, it would now require a new billing logic to only charge you for 15 days for your first month; and then do it on the first of every future month.

Managing Pricing Operations

I am not a fan of CPQ. What we did to get around CPQ was to have an online Google Sheet to calculate. It just literally lists out every single price point and MTU podium, and our salespeople just use that. When they need to make up a quote, they go there, figure out the price, and all of the back and forth with the customer happens off the Google Sheet. Finally, when they're ready to submit an actual contract, they go into CPQ and put in the details.

Natalie Louie: Pricing with Complex Underlying Costs at Oracle

Natalie Louie is a pricing guru and is currently Sr Director of Product Marketing Strategy at Zuora. She is also a pricing SME with Impact Pricing, LLC.

I spoke to Natalie about her time at Oracle. As the head of Oracle Marketing Cloud's (OMC) Pricing Strategy and Operations from 2015 to 2018, Natalie Louie has extensive experience in value creation through creative subscription pricing and packaging strategies. Her innovative strategies made it easier for customers to buy Oracle products, as well as for the sales team to sell and drive more revenue, profits and lifetime value. She elaborates on some of the innovative price changes made during her time with Oracle, and more.

The content of the sections below consists of direct quotes.

A Case Study in Re-Pricing Mobile Messaging

There is one pricing journey during my time at Oracle that stands out, it would be in the mobile space. This was a while back when smartphones were dominating, and everyone was moving towards a mobile-first world. The mobile and SMS space is a complicated domain, with many people controlling cost and distribution.

Let's say you are a company kicking off a mobile marketing campaign and you send a text message to your customers, who have opted in, with a coupon to shop on your website. That message travels through third-party aggregators, then to the telephone company (like T-Mobile, Verizon or AT&T and ultimately to the customer's smartphone. The telephone companies set the price for sending that text message and the aggregators mark it up.

So, you don't completely own pricing. There are several people taking a piece of that pie, and you have to consider all those costs. On top of this, every country has its own local telephone networks like Sprint, T-Mobile, AT&T and they all set their own rates for the cost of the SMS text message they send. On top of this, there are different types of SMS messages that also have different prices. Phone companies are also free to change the price of sending the various types of SMS text messages -- it's something like the stock market — pricing keeps changing and you can't predict it. Then, if text messages are being sent to phones in different countries, you have to consider foreign currency exchange rates, which are always changing too. You can quickly see how pricing anything in the mobile space becomes extremely complex and matrixed.

The challenge was — how do we work with this very complicated network of different telephone companies, aggregators, types of SMS messages and currency exchanges to ultimately set the price of one thing in a simple way for our customers?

Why Mobile Messaging Pricing Got Messy

When we priced and rolled out our first mobile product, we took on all the cost of sending a text message and marked it up to then sell and package as a subscription offering.

We were using an ERP at the time to house our price catalog and had to create a separate Stock Keeping Unit (SKU) for each unique SMS offering - so if I wanted to sell a SMS in the UK and USA, those were 2 different SKUs, if we had 2 different types of SMS messages, that's 4 SKUs. We sold these on a global basis, so you can see how quickly it added up to literally hundreds of SKUs for our mobile product alone. Layer in different aggregators with different costs to do business, which means different SKUs to track those costs and it really all just ended up being SKU explosion.

This was the easiest way to structure our pricing with our ERP. But over time, when we started managing the pricing strategy, we realized that it had become very hard to manage and make any changes to or control margins on a cost basis that kept changing. We even had to put clauses in our contracts that said we could change pricing on our customers if our hard costs changed too dramatically -- that's a whole different story with our sales teams and customers.

We priced mobile messages sent in each of these countries and with each of these aggregators as separate SKUs. Customers didn't like having to buy mobile messaging in each country separately. They started asking - if they send more mobile messages to one country than another, then could they apply unused credits from one country to another.. Alternatively, they had unused email messages they purchased, and asked if they could apply unused emails to send more mobile messages. Given the cross-channel world their end customers live in, they couldn't always predict if they would end up sending more mobile or email messages and didn't know how many to buy each of them.

Further, there were different costs for text messages a company initiates and for text messages a end-customer initiates (like when you opt-in for a coupon or have a text conversation). Given you can't control when an end-customer may text you, it adds to the unpredictable nature of how much text messaging should one commit to and buy?

One issue that also surfaced, our sales reps were discounting our mobile SKUs heavily. Given they didn't understand all the complex hard costs, oftentimes their discounts caused us to be in the red on many deals and not profitable with our mobile product. In some cases, we were basically paying customers to use our mobile product. We need a new pricing strategy that would ensure better margins and profitability for the long-term, while making it easier for our customers to buy our mobile product and easy for sales to sell.

Another issue was our messaging and positioning -- our value was to provide our customers the ability to send cross-channel marketing messages across any channel, whenever they wanted, but our pricing didn't reflect this. In part, because mobile messaging had so many complex, moving, costs, rules and regulations that differed from country to country -- and we were passing that complexity onto our customers. We had to work with the limitations of our ERP and decided we ultimately needed to make product changes in a way that we are no longer passing on the complexity of our mobile product to the customer. The experience of how the customer purchased and used these messages, needed to be easy. We knew we needed to do some hard work behind the scenes, to ensure an easier customer experience. So, we began meeting and strategizing on what to do.

The Solution: Making it Easy for Customers

Eventually, we came up with an idea — break apart the mobile messaging SKU and separate the hard costs vs. our markup and be completely transparent with our customers. Build a self-serve portal for customers to go and select the aggregators they want to work with and expose their costs. Allow customers have a picker in our product to pick the aggregator they want based on the prices they could see, and the aggregator would send a bill for their hard costs based on their usage. Then we created a new transaction SKU Oracle charged, that allows a customer to send and bundle both email and mobile marketing messages.

By rolling this structure out, we were able to charge the same fee for sending a message — across any channel. Customers could now send an email or an SMS message, whatever they wanted — and just pay the same fee. As a customer, you were just buying a bucket of interactions and could control your overall usage better. You needn't have to worry about controlling your usage across different marketing channels.

We also removed the burden of managing the hard costs that we couldn't control, by allowing aggregators to charge customers directly. We gave full transparency to the customer, but in a really easy way so that they could see what the costs of business doing were. Usually, complex expenses are not exposed when bundling many hard costs and margins into 1 SKU. Customers just keep negotiating because they just see one price and don't realize all the third-party hard costs. We needed to expose those hard costs and do it in a self-serve way and ended up building (almost) a marketplace for aggregators to come in and list their hard costs along with additional detail so customers could understand what value they were getting for the costs. Then, customers could pick their own aggregator themselves and be invoiced by the aggregator directly.

And then, with Oracle, they would pay for one single usage fee, like Cost Per Message (CPM) — for any marketing message sent across any channel they wanted. By exposing the hard costs of the mobile channel, we were able to bundle all our other offerings that didn't have such complex hard costs. And this ultimately made our mobile product profitable.

Convincing Management to Embrace the New Process

Pricing simple and elegantly is like the Holy Grail. When we came up with a new mobile pricing strategy, I had to work with product managers and engineers because it required a change in our products and would require a re-architecture of product areas of our mobile offering.

So, we got a lot of pushback. **That's the hard thing with pricing— you can come up with all these great ideas, but it gets hard to actually implement and build it. So, how can you build new tools if you can't use existing tools to actually support that? How do you convince product management?**

Over time, we convinced them to do it because the PM organization committed to revenue goals. Once this happened, I made a case of how better pricing strategies directly impact revenues and profits. I showed how much additional revenue we could bring in. I had already done all the pricing analysis and calculated all the numbers my pricing strategy could impact and showed the executives who owned the revenue goals to get buy-in at the top.

I detailed how much revenue we could make and how we could ensure 100% profitability for every transaction. I did my margin analysis and showed that we would never go in the red or lose money again. I also went and pulled data on all the different mobile deals we had sold in the past, how we lost money on them and how with a new strategy we could improve all those deals.

From the outside, some of our deals had really large dollar values, but given all the high and complex hard costs -- once discretionary discounts were given, we were actually paying our aggregators more than we were collecting from the customer. The customers and sales teams had no idea this was happening.

Once I showed everyone the data, I got buy-in from executives to prioritize this and add it to the roadmap. The next thing you knew -- I got engineering resources, product managers and lead a mini scrum-like team, as a pricing owner. I had to put forth use cases and detail what we wanted to do with pricing. We were able to put it in the roadmap and six months later, build it, launch it, and work with a large network of aggregators on a new business process. It was almost two years in the making.

Suddenly, there was a whole new way of working with mobile aggregators. Soon, our engineers were getting patents on what they had built, because it was really novel. It was exciting and it also hit the press, making our customers more delighted because now they didn't have to feel like they would leave money on the table anymore. They could bundle and buy packages that allowed them to send marketing messages across any channel and not have to commit usage in silos.

They could now pay one price and apply it to usage of many features, versus having to buy different SKUs for each product. And, they had full transparency on the aggregator hard costs and were invoiced by them directly in easy and seamless way

Natalie's General POV on Packaging

Companies often start with one offering, then start creating add-ons. Then you start bundling your add-ons and new features to create different packages to serve different market segments -- eventually to get to a version of Good, Better, Best packaging. You can still have add-ons and over time move the add-ons into the packages and vice versa.

Within packaging, we see the companies that are growing the fastest also package in usage SKUs, which are based on consumption or event data you are collecting. Usage-based pricing is very fair, and your customers only pays for what they use.

Depending on what type of product you have or if you are B2B, B2C or B2Every, you have to test and iterate to find the right balance of usage pricing to introduce. On average though, the benchmarks show that having 25% of your revenue come from usage-based pricing is a healthy mix to maximize your growth. And there can sometimes be too much usage pricing which can also lead to slower growth. Many companies start with looking at their existing data, products and services and can simply start out with a 'good' package.

At one of the smaller start-ups, I was with, we just had one package, which we started with. Later, we introduced a more robust package because customers started growing with us. They were outgrowing what they were habituated to using and we created a bigger package to increase our Average Selling Price (ASP).

Over time, as we moved upmarket, we decided we wanted to go back to our roots and service the start-ups that we used to work with. And then, we created a smaller package. When your package keeps growing, you create a bigger one, and then sometimes you go backwards and create a smaller package again. I have seen this motion a lot, when I was at Responsys, Hired and now at Zuora with all our customers.

While all of this is a good problem, you also have to think about whether you as a business want to go after those smaller companies again or keep it Enterprise. You have got to figure out what your target segment is and where to put your resources. But one thing is for sure — each market segment you're serving needs to have the right packaging, pricing metrics and price points (including discount strategy) that delivers value to them.

The Challenges with Pricing Operations

Pricing strategy is one thing, pricing operations another. For me, at least, the former is the easy part. In pricing operations, you face a lot of "no", and "our systems can't do this or that".

This is part of the reason I joined Zuora— I was tired of people saying 'No' to me.

At Oracle, and other startups I worked with, we were using Enterprise Resource Planning (ERP). ERPs are basically built for one-time sales. You sell the product, then you mark it up with your margin and you sell it. It works beautifully for one-time sales.

But now, when you enter the world of recurring revenue models where the customer is at the center of a new business model -- who is buying your product on a monthly or annual basis, buying based on usage, buying more, buying less or putting things on pause whenever they want -- the linear processes of an ERP break down. Making pricing changes based on how your customer wants to buy kicks off a six month or more customization project to your ERP. ERPs don't understand a subscription business model where you have multiple customer touch points and pricing strategies based on value, usage, percentage based pricing, customizable pricing metrics or unique complex billing scenarios, etc... Zuora understands all of this out of the box and was purpose built for subscription businesses. When I worked with an ERP, I had to write use case stories, be mindful of many system limitations, work with PMs and Engineers and wait 6 months until my new subscription pricing changes went live. With Zuora, these updates are achieved in clicks, not customizations.

I see two common tech stacks in the pre-Zuora world:

1. Are you using an ERP? It's just going to be a lot of customization and change orders, and there's not going to be any flexibility to launch and automate the pricing strategy and billing scenarios you want quickly.

2. Or it's a lot of manual spreadsheets and human error. I've lived in this world of manual spreadsheets, working with teams in the US and even across Europe and India to manually crunch numbers, normalize data and aggregate it back together in order to get my pricing and billing out the door.

Part of my reason I joined Zuora was because I was a subject matter expert, I am the ideal use case. I have spent my career "Frankensteining" the entire pricing process together - where I was stitching together people doing some work in manual spreadsheets, plus some customizations and change orders. And then having to wait for six months until my new pricing was ready to launch! And this is just launching pricing -- I'm not even talking about billing yet.

I used to tell all product managers on my team that I would need six months to a year for a big pricing change. I would ask them to not even begin architecting or building a product until we talk, because if there's usage, I need to be able to track the data and feed that back to the customer. Customers are going to get a bill based on the usage and have questions about it. You have got to make sure the customer can access their usage data and tie it back to their invoice, so they know they are being charged correctly.

Additionally, one critical area is also revenue recognition (rev rec). You don't want to set off any rev rec red flags. In fact, sometimes, rev rec is the first meeting I have, to understand what the rules are, because their policies and language are black and white and there isn't much room for interpretation. If you don't get rev rec right, your entire pricing strategy can fall apart. I've got horror stories about this done wrong and gone bad too, we'll save that for another time. Rev rec has to be one of your main stakeholders, along with legal, contracts, billing, quoting, payments, collections, all the up and down stream processes the office of the CFO oversees.

Choosing the Right Tech Stack for Pricing

Any pricing practitioner needs something like Zuora to own their pricing catalog, one more reason why I joined the company.

For instance, if a competitor gives a similar feature away for free that we currently charge for; I may want to bundle it now because the feature is table stakes. I may need to make those changes in real time and be able to capture that usage and manage the whole life cycle. I may want to move from a fixed annual fee to a usage based one. I want the freedom of pricing agility and not wait 6 months to roll out competitive pricing decisions. Zuora allows me to make pricing changes out of the box and send my bill out in an automated manner.

A typical best-in-class tech stack I see is one where you've got your Customer Relationship Management (CRM), and then you've got Zuora for all of your recurring revenue pricing strategies and subscription lifecycle management. And, if you have a Quickbooks or an ERP, Zuora sends your subscription data into there to run your GL (general ledger).

Zuora takes all the recurring revenue and is doing all your subscription rev rec in real time, and then inputs it into your ERP. This is because Zuora can handle usage data, complex subscription billing scenarios, charge models, collections, payments and tax that are part of a recurring revenue model business. They also have a huge ecosystem and integrations with partners to support all use cases a company needs.

To have a success subscription pricing strategy, you need a recurring revenue platform that can handle all these pricing iterations and flexibility. It's the holy grail for every pricing strategist. Because when you're thinking about value-based pricing and making sure that we're pricing according to what our customers find value in so we can keep building that recurring relationship with many different touch points, you need a platform that can handle these use cases. Technology that understands when a customer changes their mind on how they want to buy something, that we are listening for those changes and updating our pricing strategy to reflect it.

The modern day pricing operations team will function very differently than before when using a best in class tech stack. Today, I always initiate pricing strategy conversations with our PMs (Product

Managers). I'll loop in finance to do some cost and margin analysis, if relevant. Then when we have a good recommendation, we meet with a larger cross-functional pricing strategy and operations team -- , and in one meeting with our entire team, we can address all quote and order to cash collected and Rev Rec processes in one go because we are all on one tool.

Rajeev Venkat: The Move to Subscription Pricing at Verint

From a successful stint as Senior Director of Solutions Marketing, to now being Vice President of Pricing and Licensing, Rajeev Venkat is a Verint veteran.

Rajeev sheds light on the holistic switch from the perpetual license model to the subscription model across business units and product lines, and how he is leading the charge for Verint.

The content of the sections below consists of direct quotes.

The Challenge at Verint

I represent the Customer Engagement Solutions Group. We are basically focused on enhancing customer engagement or experience, such as capturing interactions across channels or modalities, analyzing them, understanding the root cause, and more recently getting into self-service channels— like interactive virtual assistants and chat bots, and more.

Given our history, we've been a traditional software company —we still have thousands of customers who have bought perpetual licenses in the past and pay maintenance for it.

But in the last three - four years, we've moved towards embracing the subscription economy, and getting people to move to the cloud.

I took over this role when the leadership realized that with all the acquisitions and the switch from the perpetual model to the new subscription one, they needed someone to look at it all holistically across business units and product lines.

We've had our transition pains. Essentially, we had to do this (the switch) quickly and aggressively, but at the same time, fit into customer cycles and their perceptions of us that have formed over the last two decades — because that's still the bread and butter for the company.

It is also not like we were a brand-new cloud-based startup that could just take off without the 'baggage' we had.

How do we manage the new businesses, and manage this with our 5,000 legacy customers?

That was the challenge. I believe we're still on the path to work through that, but we've done reasonably well over the last 18-24 months.

How Verint made the Shift

At a high level, the <u>textbook</u> approach looks at the structures that we had to put in place within our systems and processes to make the shift. This is a very theoretical understanding of things. Then there's also something I call the <u>playbook</u>, which comes out when you get into actual sales deals! I will cover both.

In terms of equating the subscription value with the older perpetual model, based on our research we said: three years of subscription price would equate to the upfront perpetual license value plus three years of corresponding maintenance fees (~18-20%) and a 3-5% annual uplift to the maintenance fee.

The above is what we call the "Term" pricing model. It is a subscription model for customers who want the option to either deploy the software in their premises, or on their own cloud. For example, large customers may have their own agreements with AWS, Azure or GCP but want the flexibility of a subscription arrangement with Verint. The Term model delivers this "Any Cloud" flexibility by allowing the customer to deploy their software on their own choice of cloud.

Obviously, if the customer is ready for the Verint Cloud, we offer the Verint Cloud SaaS pricing model. With the Verint Cloud, we add a lot more value than Term. We offload the hardware and IT costs and associated overhead that the customer would have incurred. Customers enjoy the benefits of being on the latest version of the software without having to pay for, and manage, periodic upgrade costs. Commensurate to the additional value of delivering in our cloud, the Verint Cloud SaaS price has an uplift compared to the Term price.

The second thing we had to go through, which a lot of companies probably don't have to, is to deal some rather vague licensing language and policies in the old world. In the cloud world, measurement, tracking and reporting are of paramount importance. This is because you're stressing on them, in terms of your positioning. Customers need to understand exactly how we are measuring what they see in terms of usage. Even the licensing language and our legal documents have to be a lot more transparent and simpler.

We had something called a seat-based licensing model in the past. But then, we moved to a more traditional named user — named employee-based model. This was a transition that we also had to make as part of being more transparent, easy to understand, easy to track, report and bill customers.

Then, we realized that for the SaaS train to really take off, we had to aggressively convert our installed base of customers.

We found (and we have sales tools to prove this) that we can go to an existing customer, who for instance paid us $100,000 in maintenance, that we can get up to 2x this amount as the rough average for SaaS ACV (annual contract value). This translates to $200,000 in SaaS revenue for the company moving forward if that customer moved to the cloud. We now have the tools to show customers —savings over a three or five-year timeframe, due to the offloaded hardware and IT costs.

The shift has definitely helped us by opening up markets, especially here in California, where we were not doing that well. Now, we see a complete 180-degree shift, particularly, in going after Web 2.0 or 3.0 type companies. Many of them are now Verint customers!

Without this model, we would not have had them on board. It opened up what was traditionally not a market segment for us, but has now become a big, fast-growing one.

I'll now go a bit into how we did our research, formulated our packaging and worked on pricing operations.

How Verint Surveyed and Analyzed the Customer Base

We looked at the customer base and customer advisory boards. We had representative samples of 20-40 customers across different regions. In talking to them, I also reached out to my network in the new role. We were all trying to learn as we took off.

I reached out to people who I knew in the space, and those who had worked at Salesforce, SAP, Oracle, and legacy software companies — who were either in the same boat or had just started making their cloud transition around the same time. This gave us our internal benchmarks. In coming up with the price, we took the high-level approach or formula; but we also had to look at our discount culture — as we sold through a lot of partners. In India, for instance, you have to give a 90 percent discount, which is how the procurement person feels like a champion. We looked at various things that we had done in the past, to ensure that we adjust to all of those geographic differentials too and make the necessary adjustments.

Taking a Relook at Product Packaging

We combined and offered what we call 'starter bundles,' or packages to make it easy for the customer to take the first step. This proved successful.

Salesforce or Zendesk, or any other vendors in the space – all of them have these bundled package offerings, and they assign different levels — enterprise-level, professional level, and so forth. We have that too. But I think if you're starting from scratch, these things are an absolute must.

In our case, we had a 20-year history that we had to deal with. If we had to move those customers to the cloud, they often didn't map to any models already in place. If one wanted to do a like-for-like move here, we still had to maintain an à la carte sort of combination of skills on the cloud as well.

In our case, our packages needed to offer flexibility because of all of the accommodations we continued to offer.

Interacting with Pricing and Sales Operations

A big part of what the pricing team has to do — is work actively and extensively with the 'quote desk', the order admin team, and the legal team. One of the areas where we still have an issue is in making sure that the systems, we have in place are updated. This requires a lot of investment and internal buy-in, because it's not cheap. To be honest, it is our system inadequacies that keep me up at night these days!

In many cases, the sales team also went through a lot of turnovers. Today's people are not the people we had three years ago in the field because it now takes a different skill set, dynamic and domain expertise. There was also the business aspect of training them on how the new model worked, how to present and compare it to what the customer was used to and showing them all of that from a business and a return on investment (ROI) perspective.

There was also a technical mindset change, in terms of being able to talk about benefits of the cloud. That was handled by a different team. I was more involved in coming up with the tools, and also what it meant to them. There was also a very important compensation aspect, where you had to clearly show how they were getting paid earlier, how it changed in the subscription world, and you'd still come out looking good.

The Criticality of Instrumentation & Tracking

Companies making this transition need to look at it from the product perspective, in terms of having tracking and support capabilities.

Provide customers with visibility, and also provide internal visibility to liaise with the customers.

With the cloud, there is a perception of flexibility — buy 100 today, use 300 tomorrow. But the customer needs to see it. The company's team also needs visibility so that there is no revenue leakage. This needs to be taken care of from a product perspective. The systems need to be capable of handling all that flexibility.

There will also be co-terming issues, like a customer buying 300 today and then buying another 700, four months later. How do you quote more of that, so it doesn't get too confusing for both sides? For this, **having the right billing systems to provide flexibility is essential, and it is equally important for the product to feed into those billing systems so that finance does not struggle to collect. You can sell a lot, but if you're not able to collect from customers, it's all doomed.** These are some things that companies need to watch out for, if they're making this transition.

Joshua Bloom: The A-Z of Pricing Projects at Simon-Kucher & Partners

As Managing Partner, North America, for the global strategy consulting firm - Simon-Kucher & Partners, Joshua Bloom elaborates on the pricing engagement process for SaaS companies, how it is structured, and the challenges and dogma that can potentially crop up along the way.

The content of the sections below consists of direct quotes.

Structuring the Pricing Engagement Process

There are a few hallmarks of our approach at Simon-Kucher & Partners, when it comes to structuring the process of starting a pricing engagement with any software company.

1. **Diagnostic phase:** In this phase, we develop hypotheses by looking at data — both internal transaction and usage. Along with this, we bring in pattern matching - of what has worked well and what has not, at similar companies (competitors or other software companies). We like to get it to a point where we have a strawman view of packaging, the price metric and other pricing changes that we would undertake, before we talked to any customers or prospects.

2. **Primary research phase:** We then go out to talk to customers and prospects and conduct primary research. But we're not just asking direct or open-ended questions in these conversations — we have people react to specific scenarios, often for trade-offs. At least 80 percent of projects have some type of primary research component.

The classical approach to that is conjoint analysis. It's a gold standard, but conjoint analysis is not the perfect answer for every project. It works really well when you have a certain number of features or project options to test, or when you can get a significant sample size. It works best in consumer settings and works okay in small business software settings — but it does not work very well in enterprise software settings, or the further you get down to the B2B end of the spectrum.

Different methods can be used. We use fixed trade-off screens or ask a series of probing questions. But ultimately, we're just getting reactions to some of the strawman concepts we've come up with. We'll often have a couple of different scenarios to walk people through, because that's where we start to get not just feedback, but also begin to make projections about how the market will respond. These depend on which path we go down, and what the price sensitivities may be.

3. **Implementation phase:** Once we have now found the right strategy, we think about the right implementation approach. We spend a lot of time with clients thinking through how we migrate the installed base of customers, communicate the changes, and train our salespeople to defend or uncover value. That's usually the third leg of the stool for a lot of our projects.

The time spent on the three phases ends up being pretty equal for each but depends on the research complexity level in a project. We could be doing research across multiple channels in 10 different countries for various products — it can get pretty complicated. But for a plain vanilla organization with a relatively simple product set, the time spent per phase probably looks more evenly distributed — like a month each or around that, for a month-on-month project.

Pricing Challenges Across Company Sizes/Stages

We contend with different challenges at varying stages of the company's life cycle. In the very early stages of development, a lot of questions are asked on how to price. At this juncture, companies are often still struggling with the underlying measure of pricing and what their business model looks like.

As they develop into the growth stage or become multi-product and multi-segment entities, we get a lot of questions around packaging and pricing, and how to pull together a newly complex product portfolio.

When you talk of really mature companies, we get into more of the pricing operations piece or think about discounting and channel management.

Deciding Which Pricing Structure to Use

Pricing structures can be on a spectrum — on one side, you can have a continuous consumption-based pricing structure where companies pay for what they use.

On the other end of the spectrum, it can almost be a fixed price structure sized almost using a t-shirt sizing approach M, L, XL etc. The salesperson just has to get it generally right with a generous buffer. Here the usage may be based more on the honor system.

In the middle you can have more of the cell-phone plan models, where you purchase blocks of 'usage', with incentives to move to higher tiers.

In order to select which pricing structure to use, here are a few ways which can help to decide:

1. **Predictability**: The more predictable and measurable the metric is, the more granular you can make your units and tiers (pricing variable). On the flip side, purchasing groups will always want predictability. So, if the measurement isn't as easy or the usage less predictable, in this case larger buckets with buffers might be helpful as it will deliver more cost/expense predictability to the customer.

2. **Usage Growth Rates**: Predictability is one thing, but the natural growth of the metric is another. Imagine a scenario with a rapidly growing metric — for instance with big data software, where data volume is growing exponentially for the applications

they are covering. In a cloud infrastructure model, to some degree it means that you have to get pretty granular, because your own cost structure could be under significant pressure by say month nine of a contract - if you didn't have a very granular way to charge then you face cost pressures quite fast.

3. **Correlation to Compute/Data Costs**: The third element to think about how close the structure is to the infrastructure layer versus sitting one or two steps removed — essentially, how much cost risk are you bearing? If you're just talking about something at the application layer, which is very divorced from the underlying cost structure, you can get away with big pricing buckets. The closer you get to compute and storage resources being meaningful, the more granular you have to make things.

Regarding the Good-Better-Best Packaging Structure

I'm not a believer of the dogma that the good-better-best packaging structure is a one-size-fits-all.

There are different structures, like use case packages and so on, and there are lots of different ways to think about the traditional concept of packaging or bundling functionality that aren't necessarily good-better-best. To boil it down pretty specifically, good-better-best means that there was one land-and-expand path for a customer to go through with it. It basically assumes that there is a natural level of sophistication that you can stratify your customers into, and they get there in one direction. It assumes that they start quite simple, and it is easy to say what's next with their needs.

But that is not the case with every product portfolio. Some have multiple entry points for people to start at. Others have multiple point places where they can achieve a different level of sophistication needed to go in directions B versus C - which essentially breaks the good-better-best model. We've seen often that the good-better-best model works, but not for every company, because all of them don't have one land-and-expand path.

Good-better-best also implies that the answer is in having three tiers of packaging. Again, that is not always the optimal outcome. In some companies we've worked with, a simplified two package lineup makes sense. There are others where there's one upsell path, but they need four or five tiers to cover all of the different segments of customers that they're reaching. It is useful as a tool in the toolkit to be able to say that we have a playbook for how to think about good-better-best and set limits and fences between the packages — but it's not the only packaging decision.

Our research shows that less than half of all SaaS companies have public pricing pages. If the optimal structure is not a good-better-best lineup because your product portfolio has more complexity, you're more likely to put that behind the firewall or have a salesperson walk you through it — because it's more complex. I would say that the majority of companies that do not have published pricing, are doing something other than good-better-best.

Why Companies Start A Pricing Project

I'm wary of my own selection bias because I tend to work with companies who feel that they have pricing power — but that's not always the case. In about 20 percent of projects, I work on, we're being asked to come in, because they want to get more aggressive, or try to find ways to simplify or gain share, or potentially price more aggressively and figure out how to do that in a controlled manner. The majority of companies I work with, feel that they're leaving money on the table. And we often find that they are, and their pricing elasticity is pretty low. It's a bit of a self-fulfilling prophecy — if you feel you're leaving money on the table, you probably are.

But I have seen elasticities across numerous studies that are fundamentally different than those you get in a consumer study. One of the benefits for Simon-Kucher & Partners is that when we take a step back, we have vertical practices across different industries. Yet, the elasticities are different. Another way to think about a proxy for elasticity is how important pricing is as a value driver, or as a purchase decision criterion.

If you do a consumer study, price is typically the number one factor for consumer-packaged goods or suchlike. But if you do the same study in B2B software, it will not be surprising to see that it becomes something like the third to seventh most important factor.

It's a proxy for saying, "Yes, pricing matters." It's not that it doesn't matter at all, but on a relative basis, I think the software industry has much more pricing power than other product types.

How to Price in a Blue Ocean Market

If you're really creating a new category, this is one place where I actually think that economic value analysis makes sense. It's a bit textbook, but it is about really understanding what value you are creating for your customers through their business outcomes, operational efficiencies, etc. and then remembering that even after you calculate all that, you still need to have a typical software return on investment (ROI) sharing those gains. Even if you calculate the entire value capture and you're able to document that, I still think you'll only get like 10-25 percent of that in pricing. This is because you need to leave a 4x to 10x ROI benefit to the customer. One thing that people miss, is that they do economic value analyses and say they've created all this value, so they need the corresponding price. Well, not really. You not only have to share gains with your customers, but also make it compelling for them to invest as well.

That's a useful framework to think about. If nothing else, the work done in putting that together, becomes your marketing collateral in discussions when there's no anchor and no differentiator. This is where you don't need to ask what your unique selling proposition (USP) is, versus your competitor's mentality for a market perspective. Instead, you think of how a new category or a new software changes your business operations. Speaking that language and gathering those numbers, really make a difference.

Resolving Bottlenecks in Pricing Operations

There are a few challenges in pricing operations that are pretty common. **One pitfall is having a discounting policy where everyone is just going through the motions — it lives on a piece of paper, but nobody follows it, or it didn't lock down in a system, but you have 99.9 percent of requests just being rubber-stamped. A well-run process will maintain some tension!** This could be in terms of different stakeholders getting involved, not just salespeople.

It could really ideally surface in escalation discussions – what are the key strategic factors that would cause us to discount in situations where we ordinarily wouldn't? is it that you're up against a different competitive set than maybe normal? Is it that you are trying to land an account where there's significant opportunity for growth in the future? You need to document what is different about this deal; you need to list out the number of units being purchased, the pricing you're testing, and the relative discount; and then get it approved. You're not really approving a number. The ideal scenario there, is that you're proving the deal strategy, or thinking of why you are deviating in a particular case. The vast majority of organizations do not have this in place. They either have nothing or they have a process that just looks like they are going through the motions. This is a big factor to consider.

The other thing from the pricing operations standpoint is that companies often create fairly robust processes around it when it comes to new product pricing. They'll have stage gate processes of how the initial list price gets approved but often forget that they should be regularly reviewing the pricing for their existing products on an annual basis. When you have a lot more information on your existing products, in some ways it should be easier and a more fruitful discussion on contemplating pricing change.

Configure-Price-Quote (CPQ) Systems

Some CPQ tools are an overkill for software companies, too. I've dealt with companies where they have 100 Sellable items and need a CPQ tool to be able to capture the levels of complexity and come up with the right quote. But by and large, the more common challenge I would attribute to those companies (and what I've seen from those companies asking for help with) is - doing away with 100 Sellable items, and maybe taking a more structured packaging approach to turn them into 12-15 packages, at the most. This is enough so that you don't need to use CPQ anymore, but you just need really good marketing and discovery material for your salespeople to train them on the different options.

Which Companies Need Consulting Firms for Pricing?

This may be a bit of a controversial answer, but actually **large public companies often have teams devoted to pricing and do a very good job with it. To some degree, the highest leverage we have is getting in with earlier stage companies, where we really usually have the pricing experience to turn the knobs on their business model — and the returns can be huge. It can transform the trajectory of the company, at a point when it is fairly unknown.**

If you're a large public company, you sort of know where the ship is headed. If you're a startup, you still have to deal with how much more equity must be raised, how much dilution will be faced, what the business model looks like, and what the revenue rate is going to look like, say in two years.

If we get in early, we have a really strong ability to change the trajectory of the company, which I find rewarding and I think others do as well. To be blunt, usually the first pricing is set by the founder of the company — but most such founders are technology experts. They are technology founders. So that is usually another key point — what is the first inflection point where the founder is willing to give up a little control or look at outside advice and say, "I set this based on research that I did a few years ago when we were first launching. But now that we have a robust product and we've proven product-market fit, what is next in monetization?"

Mehul Sahni: Moving to a Subscription Pricing Model at Rubrik

As the Principal Product Manager, Pricing & Packaging Strategy at Rubrik, Inc.; Mehul Sahni has been leading the charge to usher in a subscription-based pricing model in a legacy technology market. Before Rubrik, he has been in similar roles at companies like PSafe Technology and Drop.

Mehul spoke to me about Rubrik's move from Perpetual Licensing to a Subscription Pricing model as well as his general POV on rolling out pricing changes effectively

The content of the sections below consists of direct quotes.

Rubrik's Shift from Perpetual Licensing to Subscription Pricing

The backup and recovery industry has been around for decades, and not really received the advantage of modernization from today's technology — because all in all, it's a pretty unsexy thing, having database admins set up service level agreements (SLAs) to back up your data from the data center and then recover it.

Incumbents in this industry tend to sell multiple hardware products, with multiple pieces of software sold on top of this hardware, leading to multiple renewals and price changes. These make it difficult to consume and manage product, and also lead to unpredictable costs.

But this is what this industry and its customers had been used to. It's a sticky proposition, as once you get in there and back up someone's data, you get into their data center, multiple data center sites, five-year contracts, and more. Incumbents got used to this way, and there hadn't been any disruption.

Rubrik's Chief Executive Officer (CEO), Bipul Sinha was an investor at Lightspeed and Nutanix. He had a lot of insight into converged appliances — selling one piece of hardware that already had pre-installed software, a plug-and-play appliance. Nutanix was doing this for the front end, as was VMware. Bipul saw the opportunity to do this on secondary data on the backup side — and that it could be very disruptive.

Disrupting the Market

And that's exactly what it did — Rubrik went to market with just one plug-and-play appliance already with backup and recovery software. You basically paid one inclusive price for both hardware and software. This suddenly went from incumbents offering multiple devices with different renewals to a very simplified product and also a very simplified license.

The go-to market strategy resonated really well and led to our current success. Looking forward, we're building applications on top of backup data we have for customers, such as security and compliance applications that can essentially be value-added services. 'Backup and recovery' is where we started, our competitive edge — but it is turning more into a data management platform altogether.

We originally went to market with a Perpetual Life-of-Device License as we were selling into backup admins, and our buyers were really used to buying hardware as one inclusive capital expenditure (CapEx) purchase.

In April 2019, we came out with a subscription pricing model. At this point, we had been selling our product for two-three years and had over a thousand customers completely on the CapEx model. We aimed to get new customers to start purchasing subscriptions. Once we penetrated this base, we would start thinking about how to get the existing install base to switch over.

In making this change, we wanted to make pricing comparable, with a slight premium. So, if you were buying our subscription offering

Rubrik Go for a minimum three-year subscription, we wanted to ensure this is comparable to that of a customer buying CapEx (Perpetual License) with three-year support.

There was opportunity for a slight premium here. Think about it — if you were to buy an iPhone outright, it would be cheaper than if you did a three-year lease, as there's a little premium for that cash flow. We knew we could demand a little premium going into an annual payment model. But, for the most part, we didn't want the price to be significantly higher to incentivize customers to go into a subscription.

However, the more we thought about it, it was less about the price, and more about creating a holistic program with additional benefits that were not included in the CapEx license, to incentivize customers to switch to the subscription model. If pricing is equal or close, and customers see all these other benefits and features in the subscription model, they would naturally choose to go that way.

Coming up with the Subscription Model

While overall reception was good, a key critical decision Rubrik made was to not focus only on new customers but also to remember the existing customers. The subscription model was always incremental to the CapEx one, which wasn't taken away to avoid alienating existing customers.

In the industry certain competitors have made decisions that alienated the existing install base; it leads to backlash and ultimately reintroduction of the old model.

To walk through the process that we took to get to our subscription model - we started with a six-month-long study to really understand the pain points for our customers in the backup and recovery space. This included interviews, surveys and even a conjoint study where customers put together their own pricing and packaging solutions. We provided a series of products, and had customers pick the top three they would want to see bundled together.

This in-depth customer study allowed us to realize the pain points:

1. **High upfront costs** with CapEx.

2. **Cloud migration** — Chief Information Officers (CIOs) mandating teams to migrate X percent to the cloud within three to five years. So, they want to make sure the license model they're purchasing will future proof them for the cloud.

3. **Unpredictability** around costs, specifically related to hardware refreshes.

Once we found these pain points, we needed to create a subscription program to tackle them but keep pricing relatively in the same range as the CapEx model. If we resolved the issues, we thought hopefully everyone will start choosing this option naturally over the CapEx model.

The solutions:

1. **Annual Pay:** Our subscription gave the option of prepaying all upfront, or an annual payment option..

2. **Future-proof:** We also included license transferability between the hardware appliance and the cloud for the period of the term, to eliminate worries of futureproofing, eliminating double charges for using our software to deploy to the cloud.

3. **Free refreshes:** Lastly, for complicated refreshes or unpredictable costs, we decided on an evergreen hardware refresh program — as long as you continued to renew every three years, you'd be eligible for a free hardware refresh. Essentially, if you bought Rubrik today on subscription, you would not have to worry about paying for hardware again.

All these benefits were discovered through the customer research phase, where we also asked about willingness to pay, how much they would be willing to pay more than the annual payment model, etc.

Enabling Sales to Succeed

Sales enablement and Total Cost of Ownership (TCO) building is a very critical piece to pricing and packaging. I view my role similar to that of a product manager, but the only difference is that my product is a licensing vehicle. I research my license and then make a roadmap for the first one. If there's going to be a second product, I work on the upgrade license. I have to take this roadmap to the market and ensure that everybody understands how to sell it and understands its value — both customers and the field. Then, I also have to follow all the success metrics and tracking.

We learned quickly (as soon as we launched) that the field was starting to do a TCO positioning the CapEx model and Go model to the customer at the same time. This ends up confusing customers and slowing down the deal. If you show both models, the customer is bound to ask for a TCO for both. Its important to lead with one option based on the customer needs.

In this way, we make a Go/No-Go table. We position one model at a time, do one TCO at a time. The majority of the time Rubrik Go would satisfy it, but in some edge cases, it doesn't. Some at Rubrik who have earlier sold SaaS and subscription at peers like Snowflake or ServiceNow, got this point easily; but others who had to switch over, came from companies with older pricing models — places like Dell, EMC and more. Getting these lifers in the backup and recovery market to buy into the vision and positioning of Rubrik Go as the main option took some time. We learned from this and made it part of our pricing and packaging enablement and go-to-market for all other offerings thereafter.

Selecting Pricing Value Metrics

Since we were still selling appliances, we didn't really need to mess with the metric for the hardware much and it remained tied to raw backend terabytes.

Selecting the value metric actually comes more in play with our SaaS products. That has no hardware involved. For instance, we have Office 365, other workloads, security or compliance products that we may be pricing as not included in our base product. In those scenarios, it's more strategic to get the metric right. **People think Pricing & Packaging** is mostly about determining the correct price, but what metric you price on, **how you package it and what's included — that requires more strategic rationale.**

We first set the baseline and figured out the most comparable market in the industry, how they price, and the overall market consensus feedback. For example, Office 365 backup products include Veeam, Commvault, Metallic, AvePoint: and also, just a Microsoft subscription. All that products are price on a $ per user per month metric — all charge on the same metric because that's how Microsoft charges.

The general consensus from the market and customers is that this is a very easy metric for them to digest. Their employees are users, and they know how many employees they have, how many they're backing up, and the all-inclusive price for that. They're trained on purchasing on that metric since that's how they buy their Microsoft Office 365 subscription.

There are clear indicators in this situation that the market is trained in purchasing this way. If you were to purchase on a completely different metric, it could be disruptive or counterproductive to your offering. There might be other examples where it could be really expensive.

Let's say you have a DR (Disaster Recovery) product, which charges $700-900 per virtual machine (VM). A lot of people say that gets really expensive, so they only end up protecting 20 percent of workloads that are mission-critical versus the entire environment. This could be an opportunity for disruption because the feedback is that the licensing model is somewhat prohibitive to protect 100 per cent of an environment.

All this is an indicator of what the market is doing and if one can do something different that simplifies the licensing model... Could it be an all-inclusive, unlimited offering to make it easier for the consumer?

Lastly, when you get to price, you want to benchmark your product compared to the competitors.

To take the earlier DR example and pricing, if you have another DR competitor— you have to be honest and synced up with your product team. The question is how developed the product will be at initial roll-out versus a year or two from then, compared to competition. If your product is comparable then your street price should be relative to them for a similar environment.

Differences between Commercial and Enterprise Pricing

Do we think about packaging differently when it comes to certain customers or verticals? We definitely have different license models for commercial and enterprise customers. It all comes down to understanding your customer and how they want to purchase.

For Rubrik, commercial customers still really enjoy just a Rubrik appliance experience — shipping, plug, and play. Enterprise customers think about other things — having a software-only solution to deploy on hardware or on third-party hardware they want to stick to. They have other needs that our commercial license wouldn't meet.

We have different licenses available for enterprise customers, as they typically demand more Enterprise License Agreement (ELA) type offerings, where they want to pick from all software offerings or want all-inclusive ones — an all-you-can-eat or deploy option for any hardware they want. They demand a lot more flexibility in what products they're going to use or are entitled to. They also have other requirements, from discounting to pricing. So, our enterprise licensing model allows for some of that. With commercial customers, it's really about go-to-market velocity and simplicity, and just getting the transaction done really fast, having them ready to go.

But commercial and enterprise might not be the only way to look at it. It also comes down to your sales motion, and if that is different or customer needs are different, you can adjust packaging and licensing to allow for sales motion to happen more seamlessly.

Enterprise customers	Commercial customers
Demand more ELA type offerings *Want to pick from all software offerings or all-you-can-eat variants* *Need more flexibility in products they're entitled to* *Have more in-depth requirements from discounting and pricing*	*Mainly enjoy the appliance experience* *Need go-to-market velocity* *Want simplicity* *Prefer to get a transaction done quickly*

The Need for a Customer-Centric Outlook

The key takeaway is you need something to incentivize your customer to choose subscription over CapEx. **We often see competitors just go out with the same model versus the CapEx, and it looks very self-serving. Customers think they're trying to just show more subscription revenue to get a higher IPO valuation. What's in it for the customer?**

The goal in such a situation is to make it abundantly clear to the customer to choose a specific **program**, and not think of it as a license or a choice over a CapEx model.

That's the customer-centric takeaway. The other is understanding who your field or sales organization is and knowing who to rely on with a background of selling subscriptions, who you can make an internal brand ambassador for your subscription program. Start tracking the sales team members doing well with this model, bring them in, ask questions and have them tell success stories to their teams. It needs to come from within. This is when you start seeing real traction and conversion.

Jan Pasternak: General Pricing & Packaging Perspectives

Jan Pasternak is a recognized leader in the sphere of Software Pricing & Packaging and has driven pricing for companies such as Microsoft, LinkedIn, Citrix and Coupang.

From growing revenue through optimizing product line-up to managing sales policies, Jan's ideas tap into a deep understanding of the subject.

I interviewed Jan on his approach to software pricing, where he shared his general approach to the topic and some lessons learnt while he was leading pricing at Citrix.

The content of the sections below consists of direct quotes.

Lessons from Citrix: Pricing an Established Product

When Jan joined Citrix around 2014, the focus was initially on how to approach the portfolio across the existing product range. While the key product at the time was GoToMeeting, there were a variety of other communication products like GoToWebinar and GoToTraining, besides other security and remote access products also on SaaS. Jan's job was to redo the pricing for all of them, embarking on a successful journey to grow revenue through optimizing product line-up and managing sales policies.

The following are some key perspectives in his own words:

In the beginning, the sales of all our products at Citrix combined both offline (in-person) and online. The challenge was different for each, but some themes in SaaS products were common.

Usually, for established/mature products, core functionality tends to get commoditized. Larger players like Microsoft, Amazon, and Google, started providing a product for free — like videoconferencing with Google, or a single sign-on with Microsoft Office 365 that is either free or heavily discounted.

Such functionality was initially offered by independent companies like Okta, GoToMeeting or GoToMyPC — and then, they became part of a commoditized body of product.

The company has to understand how to adjust the line-up as it could become too expensive — but it also has to stay competitive and provide core functionality at either a premium or very low cost.

In this case, the key is to focus on the premium elements and figure out how to make money on them. A company specializes in a certain feature, whether videoconferencing, password management or single sign-on. They probably have much more advanced premium features that they can offer — which Google, Microsoft, the Ankle Biters or the competition are not offering.

The goal or challenge for products that are already established and being commoditized is to stretch the line-up to accommodate the masses, who are just interested in basic functionality. At the same time, you also have to push some portion (whether five or seven percent) into premium offerings, which the company specializes in.

Enhancing Packaging Differentiation

To talk about a differentiated feature based on which one could create a premium tier, let's take the example of GoToMeeting. Here, the differentiated feature was whiteboard functionality. We considered introducing some GoToWebinar functionality into it. So, you could run large, all-hands-on meetings from your GoToMeeting or incorporate it into other communication, including email, chat, and messaging systems.

This means you're not just selling the fact that one can talk over video, like Zoom, but the premium of making scheduling easier. For instance, adding the scheduling functionality of everybody marking an available time, and the most suitable time for all to meet is automatically chosen.

Jan's Approach to Pricing Projects

When it comes to general pricing methodology, I have observed that there are three stages that work best.

You must first start with a hypothesis around key value drivers, customer preferences and product packages.

1. **The Data Stage:**
    a) You start by doing/undertaking competitive landscape research
    b) You then understand what the customers need and want, and what they declare. Ask customers to volunteer information and send them surveys. These can take different forms, such as the Van Westendorp analysis. In-person interviews can be conducted to qualitatively assess pain points and expectations.
    c) All of this should help inform/revise your key hypothesis.
2. **The Testing Stage:** The next phase is testing. You try to do A/B testing or take a similar approach. In some cases, it may not be possible to split the website into two! But then, you might try to test on two different cohorts of prospects, and offer them slightly different tiers, within different packages. Typically, in such cases, we see that what customers actually do during tests is directionally similar to the results of the research, surveys and studies — but the net impact can also be different. E.g., In one test, we expected a 50 per cent greater 'take rate' for a certain tier, but in practice or in testing, it was only 20 per cent greater, or then 70 per cent greater. The intensity can vary.

The round of testing usually leads you to polish the new offering. You validate the key value drivers you selected in the beginning, but now you understand better what the tiers should be. There could be two or maybe four, and you can also determine the cut-off points between the tiers in order to maximize revenue.

In testing, data simplicity matters. If you propose four tiers of a product, even if that means each prospect finds a solution better suited to their needs and consumption, the tiers can get confusing as they require analysis to choose. If you offer fewer tiers, even if they don't fit the customer needs as well, you see a higher conversion rate. This is a bit counter-intuitive initially.

It is important to not test only on the customers who are already visiting your website. A common mistake is putting something on a website without a broader demand generation campaign — especially when it comes to discounts. If you're only talking to pre-existing customers, and offer them the product they visited the website for, but cheaper? Of course, they will buy it!

But one cannot quite measure if you will be able to attract new customers who are not even considering the products. It could lead to false negatives and misplaced comfort.

It must be added that driving agreement across departments is necessary. If you are introducing discounts, finance will be terrified; sales will have mixed feelings — because on the one hand, they can sell something more easily, but on the other, they cannot meet quotas if the discount is too deep. The product team will probably be excited to connect to more users. Driving the agreement on what the success metric is, and ensuring that everybody is comfortable with that, is more difficult than doing the data work.

3. **The Controlled Launch Stage:** Once you have iteratively tested changing the tiers and found the optimal line-up, you do a release that is very controlled and limited to a small portion of your prospects or customers. Even at the last stage, some corrections may be needed. You don't want to do a big release after stage one or two — inch out to the market with incremental, restricted releases. This is why it is all quite a time-

consuming and engaging process. But overall, it provides you with the best quality of results.

Harnessing Surveys Effectively

Multiple conversations with customers face an issue will not amount to much, due to difficulties in quantifying such results. How do you design the right survey, then? Factors to consider include designing the right survey with the right financial model and being data-driven by capturing different tiers' perception or performance.

The challenge in coming up with a new tier and running a survey is that it requires the customer to know your offering and value propositions. You may need to provide considerable context before running through the simulation and give out information about what the customers are selecting in a survey. This is why it's potentially difficult to get people to complete a survey, and you often have to incentivize them to get to the end.

Rolling Out Changes Carefully

When you have a new product, you can test more ideas as you don't have a well-established customer base to be careful about. For us, most of the products under consideration still had a large body of subscribers, who should not be rushed too much.

How you change the line-up but not cannibalize revenue from the existing customer base, is a whole different chapter. You could increase attractiveness of a product and boost new sales, but risk losing some existing customers, from ongoing or recurring subscriptions. The key here is to be proactive about change, let it happen on your terms, rather than having a displeased customer contact you.

Balance this with segmenting the existing customer base and offering slightly varying things to different cohorts. Some use the product very often; some got a deep discount when they signed up, as they negotiated well. Some bought 100 seats and are using 7; others are using 70.

Considering all the variables, one needs to segment the customer base and vary the approach. Proactively and creatively offer alternatives. Stay upfront on prices going down and offer either a better option for the same money, like an upgrade, or a discount (with some strings, not unilateral concessions), like committing to more time or getting an add-on.

It also helps to create a new line-up and modify it to be quite different from the old one. Taking the same tiers and discounting them makes the comparison too easy for the customer. Even purely from a marketing perspective, packages should be called something different, like changing 'Pro' and 'Elite' plans to 'Premium' and 'Advanced', with variances in the feature set.

Identifying the Right Value Metric

Two important elements to consider before addressing the difficulty in selecting an actual pricing model (like charging by number of seats, per interaction, data-volume driven, etc.) are:

1. **What is the customer accustomed to:** The most important thing is to recognize and acknowledge what customers are used to. I tried using a pricing model like cost per action, instead of a flat rate, with the view that it would be more beneficial to the customer — and they didn't like it because that's not what they were used to. Being overly creative sometimes backfires.

2. **Demonstrate return on investment:** This is the most difficult and alluring part in enterprise sales. The closer the pricing is related to the movement of customer money, the easier it is to sell. These are flexible pricing models that take a cut from the revenue.

Pricing is not necessarily always about what objectively generates the highest revenue.

PRICE TO SCALE

Think American Express — they don't own terminals, but just the standard, and make huge amounts of money for something like payment rails. But because they collect the money, when the customer makes money, there is no pushback, and their fees are paid — because there is no risk.

On the other hand, look at inexpensive Office solutions, for $9.99 or $19 a month. People question whether they will make enough interaction in that value, to justify the commitment of purchasing for a year.

That becomes a big conversation on how the customer wants to be charged. The more flexible, the better. The company, whichever round of financing it is in, should demonstrate to shareholders or investors that it has a stable source of revenue. Illustrating this is easier if you can demonstrate subscriptions and committed customers.

Kevin Christian: The Move to Consumption Pricing for IT Infrastructure Software

Software related to IT infrastructure and Operations Management has been historically priced based on hardware or asset size under management, be it the number of processors, the size of the storage or the amount of data transferred. In this model, a customer would buy a license for a particular size and then try to stay within the license limit. The vendor would also struggle to ensure that the customer did not use anything more than what the license permitted. Sometimes this is enforced with license keys that are different to administer and not user friendly.

Public cloud providers like AWS and Azure heralded a new approach with architectures that allowed their customers to provision hardware and software in a granular and elastic manner. This model has since been taken up by many providers of hardware and software.

While this movement has been natural for SaaS providers, there are interesting variations that occur when the same methods are applied to hardware, as well as services tied closely to hardware.

Kevin Christian, presently with Infoblox, is an industry leader with a wide exposure to pricing strategy and operations. Since 1997 he has run the pricing function at several companies who are leaders in their own industry segments. From 2008 to 2013 he ran his own consulting business with the same focus area. Through his long presence in the industry, he has been witness to the transition of the IT infrastructure industry from a licensing regime to a consumption/metered one.

In the following sections we share Kevin's insight on both his general principles for pricing success as well as a fictionalized case study of NewCo and its transition to consumption pricing.

The content of the sections below consists of my summary from our interview and is not a direct quote.

General Principles for Pricing Success

Organizing the Pricing Program

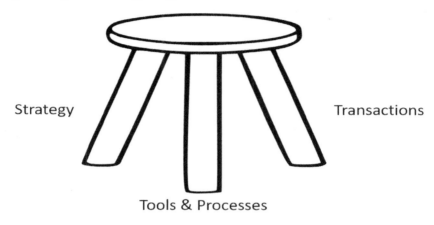

Strategy

Transactions

Tools & Processes

Fig. 33: The Three Legs of the Pricing Stool

Per Kevin, at most software companies you can break down a Pricing Program into three big areas, or legs so to say (see Figure 33). The first leg is Strategy which includes programs and policies, financial analysis, market analysis, and competitive analysis. Typically, the changes are planned as short term, say over 6 to.12 months, and long term over the coming 2 to 5 years.

The second area is pricing of specific or individual Transactions. The elements here are what is often referred to as the Deal Desk. The activities in this area are about approving non-standard discounts on special, large deals and any non-standard contract terms.

The third area is Tools and Processes. This consists of processes set up for reviewing prices and setting new prices or changing existing prices. Also covered in this group are activities like publishing the price list, setting up SKU's - it is any system related changes and whatever the quoting process is.

Getting the model right

The pricing model consists of the pricing metric, the list prices, and the volume discounts and rules around how the price is applied. The pricing metric is a part of the pricing model. The pricing metric is the quantity you count in order to come up with a price. It could be user, CPU, Mbps, GB/day, it could be anything that makes sense for the particular solution being sold. For a pricing metric to be successful, it has to have three attributes - Simple, Measurable, and Scalable.

- The Simple attribute implies that one can explain the pricing metric during an average elevator ride. This is very important because many companies cannot. This is the kind of attribute that VC's care for deeply. No one has time to spend on 10 slides explaining the pricing model - at best it can be one or two slides.

- The Measurable and Scalable attributes are related to each other. In the SaaS world, Measurable means that you should be able to count or measure whatever you are charging for. For example, it serves no purpose to price on a per user basis if you do not have the ability to count unique users by, for example, unique login IDs for users.

- The Scalable attribute means the ability to capture more returns from a customer when the perceived value for the customer scales. A large company or company that gets a lot of value from the solution should pay a relatively higher price, and a small company or company that gets less value from the solution should pay a lower price.

Beyond these essential three, we can list four more attributes to ascertain if the pricing model is effective:

- The fourth attribute we can add is Predictability, as seen by the customer. The customer wants to be able to budget, so they want to be able to predict how much they'll have to pay and when.

- The fifth attribute is Flexibility, which means having the ability to adjust for unusual use cases.

- The sixth attribute is whether it is operationally easy to implement in terms of the tools you have (e.g., Salesforce or CPQ or another commercial platform). This is an internal consideration, not form the point of view of the customer.

- The seventh attribute is Fairness, as seen by the customer. For example, a pricing metric might be perceived as unfair if it is a percent of the customers revenue. It might make sense to you as the vendor to charge this way, but a customer is unlikely to be willing to pay this way, because they might perceive the pricing as unfair.

The Story of NewCo: Evolution to a Consumption Model

To get an industry-wide perspective, Kevin alludes to an imaginary company that can be called Newco Assets and Operations. This company has offerings in the complete infrastructure space - from networking, IT asset management (ITAM), IT operations, and automation (ITOA) to Information Security. This is a fairly typical profile for companies in this space.

Traditional IT Infrastructure and Operations software was deployed on physical systems that were mostly on-premises, where the vendor was far removed from physical access, and customers bought licenses to match the specifications of their infrastructure.

With this pricing, the pricing was anchored by the hardware-oriented deployment model, where the customer paid a small price for software running on a smaller machine and a higher price for the software running on a bigger machine.

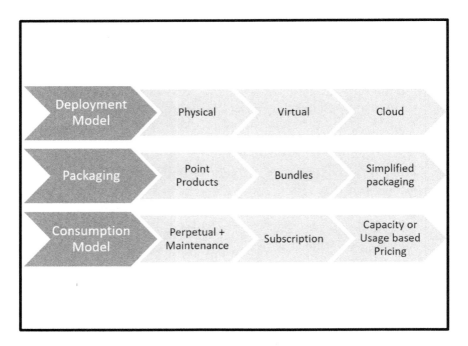

Fig. 32: The Evolution of Pricing from Perpetual Licensing Models

However, with cloud computing, this model is changing, and so is NewCo's Pricing. As shown in Figure 32, the evolution can be described using three dimensions of the problem, each having an impact on packaging:

- **First,** the deployment model has changed over time. Software used to be deployed at first on a physical device then moved to be deployed on virtual devices and eventually moved to being in the cloud.

- **Second,** is the packaging. A company such as Newco may start off with one or two point products. Then, if they are successful and grow, they end up with many point products until they get to the point where there are too many point products at which point, they start creating bundles. Further down the road they end up with too many bundles which turns out to be confusing for their field and channel partners. Eventually, they get to a point where they realize that they have to simplify the packaging.

- **Third,** is that metric on which customers are asked to pay for is also changing. In the beginning, it used to be a perpetual license plus annual maintenance charge. Then it became a subscription. And now it is moving to more of a meter style pricing - like what AWS or Azure do today - where it is based on some kind of a capacity or usage-based metric.

In NewCo's case its packaging had grown very complex with the addition of many point products and the company moved to a simpler packaging structure. In its case it reverted back to a Good, Better, Best style of packaging. *(This is something we've covered earlier in the book.)*

It starts with a small (or Good) package which is the minimal viable product that creates value for a customer. The medium (or Better) sized package is designed for the vast majority of customers. Finally, the everything (or Best) package is for the customers with the most well-defined needs or the most sophisticated customers who want every single feature and function. In this model, the point products and bundles are gone, and the company is left with just those three packages. The packages are subsets of each other. The Good package is a subset of the Better package, and the Better package is a subset of the Best package.

Implications of Simpler Packaging

As part of their own packaging transition, Newco has also arrived at a GBB packaging that covers all of Newco's offerings consisting of Networks & ITAM, ITOA and Information Security. The customer can choose whichever of the three packages they want, but other than that, does not get to pick and choose individual items a la carte.

One problem in this three-level packaging is that the salespeople may like to sell an entry or lower-level package first and go back later to sell the higher one. That is because they like to sell more to existing customers. To grow, the Sales team would take an ITAM customer and sell them ITOA or Information Security. Similarly, if they have an Information Security customer, they sell them ITAM or ITOA, or, if they have an ITOA customer, they sell them ITAM or Information Security. Most customers don't buy all three products initially.

For Newco, how this works out is that they now have their Good, Better and Best packages. So, if you have a customer who bought Good, Sales could later try to upsell them to Better, and if they had bought Better, Sales could late try to upsell them to Best. If the customer started with Best then there is no upsell because they are already at the top.

One way to get over this situation is to look at another approach to growth, and that is to look at the pricing metrics or variables in each of these packages. For example, Newco can use the size of the customer's network in terms of the number of nodes or endpoints. In this case, Newco can capture growth if the customer's network grows from 10000 endpoints to, say, 50000, thus scaling five times.

There is a case to be made here for still having a very small number of point products on top of the Good, Better and Best packaging. After a company has this type of packaging for a year or two they might choose introduce a small number of higher priced point products targeted to specific market verticals or specific customer needs. These products may turn out to be costly to deliver. Because they are costly to deliver, they would have to be priced high enough in order to make any money on them. In this way the Good, Better, Best model can be expanded with a small number of select point products.

Choosing the Right Pricing Metric

Taking the example of Newco, they had similar decisions to make across their Networking and ITAM, ITOA, Information Security portfolio. They had to decide whether and how to have a single usage metric and if they would need different metrics for their three offering groups.

Since the Networking and ITAM offering itself has multiple product lines, they could technically have different metrics for each of those.

Networking could be priced based on metric A, ITAM on a second metric B, ITOA on a third metric C, and Information Security on a fourth metric D.

Now if they used all of those metrics then they could either sell them separately or convert them into 10-12 bundles starting with what would be appropriate for a small attorney's office and going up to a large Walmart type of facility and then the typical corporate office of a large multi-building campus. For each bundle, they would need to specify a ceiling for the respective usage metric of each of the product components within that bundle.

So, it was apparent that this would become really quite complex and yet it would never fit exactly for any single customer; they are always going to need more of some item and less of some other. And even then, they may feel they are overpaying for something.

Even though this arrangement is complex, a number of companies price their offerings like this. One example of this could be Cloudflare[34]. As Figure 34 shows, Cloudflare has a Free plan and then Pro, Business and Enterprise plans. Then if the customer needs more they can take from a set of Add-Ons on top of these plans as depicted in Figure 35.

---

34 https://www.cloudflare.com/en-in/plans/

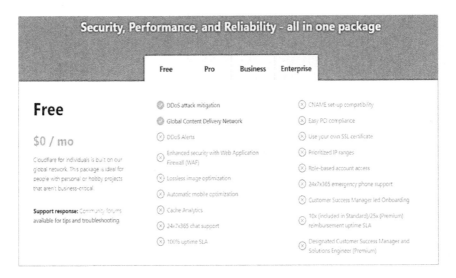

Fig. 34: Cloudflare Pricing Plans

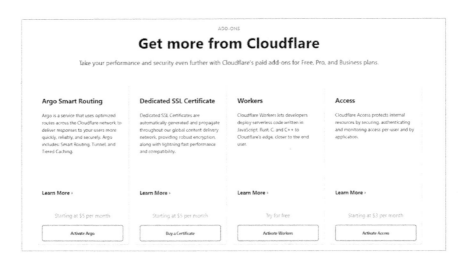

Fig. 35: Add-Ons for Cloudflare Pricing Plans

For Newco it made more sense to have a single metric for everything. Newco needed to look at what was theoretically best for them and their established sales motion. In Newco's case, they decided to go with a single metric because that was their Sales and field leadership preference and that group values simplicity more than anything else. The field leadership wants to do big deals where the customer buys all the products.

In Newco's case the single metric used became nodes or endpoints for everything, even though other different metrics would have been more natural for some of those individual items. In this case, they would be using a suboptimal metric for some of the items, but they were well advised to do it to have the simplicity of the same metric for all the items. Using this single metric, they were been able to develop the Good, Better and Best packages for each of Networking and ITAM, ITOA and Information Security.

Considerations for Rollout

At this point Newco has been over the transformation and simplification of packaging that they attempted and the single metric approach to pricing that they liked. Now they have to deal with how they roll this out to customers and their own field teams.

We start with a metric that we wish to use, and in Newco's case, it is the nodes or endpoints.

Newco has multiple ways in how they can ask the customer to pay for what they consume. The first method is a hard cap, such that the customer pays for a certain quantity and they cannot go over the ceiling. The second method is monthly billing in arrears, where the customer consumes what they need, and Newco bills them for the actual arrears based on what they consumed for a period that has been chosen, say per month. That is the method AWS and Azure use. It is also possible to bill the customer in advance for a certain amount, but instead of a hard cap it is a soft cap, or what you could call a flex model. They can go over the ceiling and at the end of the period their ceiling gets resized. This flex method has become quite popular with the large cloud vendors such as IBM, HP, and Dell, and has become a recommended model.

Having developed a mature and elegant model Newco still has the challenge of getting it implemented internally. To review the process, there are four steps to complete:

- The first is to decide the metric to price on, that being the number of nodes or endpoints for Newco.

- Next is the need to build the ability to measure the chosen metric into the product, and that is non-trivial. Product managers and engineers may have a tendency to postpone this, but it is critical to pricing success. As the person with ownership for the pricing model, you may have to drive this with the E-staff from the top down. Even then, this is quite difficult, and the actual changes may take a year or more to accomplish. The lack of instrumentation when transitioning from licensing to metric-driven subscriptions is a common phenomenon across many companies.

- The next step in implementing the model is to collect all the data into a database, or more likely, some sort of data lake.

- Finally, you have to make the data visible and put it into the hands of your customers and internal teams. This is especially important for your Customer Service Management (CSM) team. Customer service managers are responsible helping customers be successful using the product, getting customers to use features and functionality they aren't using and may not know about, and both of these activities drive follow-on sales for the field. To do this, your entire compensation model, your field model, the sales motions, the Go-To-Market (GTM) strategy, and the Sales Ops features like territory assignments have to change.

In this transformed approach, the Sales teams get compensated for upselling a customer on new functionality, or they get compensated for increasing the quantity that the customer is buying or some similar change. They don't get compensated for anything else because the CSM team has taken on most of the post-sales work. In that sense, the CSM team is fully focused on the data being generated from the selling and consumption.

The key challenge with this approach is that the CSM team cannot succeed unless they have all the data on usage being generated. Having the data ready is critical for the way we want to price now - pick the metric, count it, collect it in a data lake, show it in a dashboard. Unless we can do those four things, the new pricing model will not work. This is not a problem that is confined to one company but is prevalent quite widely. The PMM or Pricing leaders may face an uphill climb to influence Product or Engineering to prioritize this instrumentation for pricing, but it is important to get the new Pricing to actually work.

Printed in Great Britain
by Amazon

77225306R00129